Urban Hikes

Urban Hikes
IN AND AROUND
Baltimore

Mike Strzelecki

Camino Books, Inc.

Philadelphia

Printed in Canada.

1 2 3 4 5   09 08 07 06

Library of Congress Cataloging-in-Publication Data

Strzelecki, Mike, 1963-
    Urban hikes in and around Baltimore / Mike Strzelecki.
      p. cm.
    Includes bibliographical references and index.
    ISBN 0-940159-84-8 (paper: alk. paper)
      1. Hiking—Maryland—Baltimore Region—Guidebooks.
  2. Baltimore Region (Md.)—Guidebooks. I. Title.

  GV199.42.M32B347   2004
  917.52'710444—dc22   2004043615

ISBN-13: 978-0-940159-84-6
ISBN-10: 0-940159-84-8

Book design: Dana Smith
Book cover design: Jerilyn Bockorick
Back cover photograph: ©2005 Geoffrey S. Baker
Maps: Susan Tseng

This book is available at a special discount on bulk purchases for promotional, business, and educational use.

Publisher
Camino Books, Inc.
P.O. Box 59026
Philadelphia, PA 19102

www.caminobooks.com

*This book is dedicated to my wife Kelly,
who forever shows me that the world is a
rich and beautiful place.*

Contents

Introduction

Urban Hikes In and Around Baltimore is the result of two very different people entering my life a few years ago. One was Bruce Chatwin, the British travel writer and world wanderer. While browsing a used book store, I picked up a beaten and dog-eared copy of Chatwin's masterpiece, *In Patagonia*, which tells of his journey through Argentina, the "uttermost part of the earth." It was the most beautifully written and engaging piece of travel literature I ever laid eyes on. Chatwin's stylish and well-chiseled prose inspired me to put pen to paper, and his persistent infatuation with the concept of nomadism and exploration unleashed in me a desire to rove.

Then along came my daughter Zi Li, whom we adopted from China in 1997 when she was five months of age. Zi Li entered my life at a time when I was running long distances, logging many miles on mountain trails, country roads, and city streets. As the diligent parent of any infant knows, time-consuming personal hobbies like distance running defer to more mundane child-rearing chores such as diaper-changing and lunch-packing. So instead of running the streets of Baltimore, I downshifted to a walking pace and included Zi Li on my back in a child carrier. We hiked two, sometimes three times a week, each time covering five to fifteen miles through the Baltimore area's most interesting neighborhoods. We called our treks "walkabouts." And what we discovered was a fascinating city with an unusual and rich suffusion of character, architecture, culture, and ethnicity. A city ripe for hiking.

Urban Hikes In and Around Baltimore is the end product of all those walkabouts with Zi Li. It's a compendium of our favorite hikes. It features ten urban treks ranging in distance from three to over eight miles. They are through neighborhoods that are interesting, safe, and culturally rich. For each hike I provide commentary on natural and cultural history, geography, architecture, and attractions; detailed hiking directions; and a map.

The map for each hike is designed to supplement the

written directions. The route of each hike is provided on the map by a series of arrows. The start of each hike is designated by an encircled "S," and the finish by an encircled "F." The numbers along the route correspond with stages of that hike's text. Since all hikes in this book are circuitous, each has its start and finish at the same location. Short-cuts to each hike can be made by referring to the respective map.

The text for each hike concludes with a list of suggested readings to learn more about the area traversed. Much of the information included in this book was culled from these resources. Additional information was derived from other literature and websites, oral tradition, and personal observation.

At most, *Urban Hikes In and Around Baltimore* will encourage suburban and rural dwellers to explore and experience the area's many urban neighborhoods, perhaps for the first time. At least, it will provide structure and purpose to those tourists and city residents aimlessly wandering the streets of Baltimore.

One question warrants clarification: How does the urban hike differ from a walking tour? The name "walking tour" connotes a short walk in a specific neighborhood, one where every stone is overturned and every attraction is explained in detail. The urban hike, on the other hand, is a more lengthy jaunt that breezes through several neighborhoods and covers lots more ground. Commentary is given in capsule-like form—easily digestible to someone on the move. Enough to hold interest, but not enough to bog the hiker down in overwrought description. The urban hike is as much about locomotion as discovery. And, in my opinion, it's the best way to experience—not see, but experience—a city.

You may notice that this book does not provide an estimated walking time with each hike. This is because each hiker moves at his or her own pace, and each is encouraged to explore beyond the bounds provided in this book—without regard to speed or time. My guess is that Bruce Chatwin did not don a watch as he meandered his way across the Argentinean pampas. As a general rule though, the casual walker who takes in parks and window displays can count on moving at about two miles per hour. More exercise-minded hikers can plan on a three- to four-mile-per-hour pace.

The hundreds of miles that I logged in preparing this book led to several observations and suggestions that may make your hiking experience more enjoyable. They are:

Hike in the morning. The city bears a more pleasant aura in the wee hours—before the daily siege of buses and crowds. If you never thought the words "city" and "quiet" could in any way be congruous, try a Sunday morning hike. It's as if you are seeing the city come alive.

Don't leave the kids at home. The greatest pleasure I derived from writing this book was sharing the experience with my family. My one-year-old son Graham and three-year-old daughter Zi Li covered every mile with me— Graham on my back in a child carrier, and Zi Li in a baby jogger. Inluding them heightened my enjoyment, and hopefully added to their life-experience. Expose your children to the wonders of Baltimore.

Wait for spring to hike the residential neighborhoods. Communities like Annapolis and Mt. Washington are pretty in their own right. But when the azaleas and tulips are blooming, and the dogwoods are dropping white and pink petals, these communities shine.

Explore beyond the bounds. This book may appear to hold your hand, but it wasn't intended to. Baltimore is strewn with secret pearls—parks, restaurants, shops, and homes—many hidden on back streets and in obscure nooks not traversed on these hikes. Knock about the neighborhoods on your own, make serendipitous discoveries, find some of these pearls.

Eat up! Baltimore has a fantastic selection of restaurants and coffee shops (and no, I'm not referring to the cookie-cutter franchises on the suburban outskirts). Here's your chance to find and try some. The Downtown and Peninsula hikes both ascend portions of Charles Street, which is clearly the city's culinary epicenter—and a veritable gauntlet of ethnic eateries. The residential hike routes are freckled with coffee and bagel shops. And more than a smattering of discrete corner bars in East and South Baltimore beckon for bent elbows. Grab a bite as you go.

A Note on Safety

The hiker's level of safety is directly proportional to his or her degree of common sense. Cities can be dangerous, as can suburbs and rural areas. I considered safety as a prime factor when selecting hiking routes for this book. That said, you can still take measures to promote an added element of security. Hike in the daylight hours, when the streets are busier. Hike with a partner. And most importantly, if a particular street or neighborhood makes you feel uncomfortable, don't go there. Of course, city safety conditions are not static, and can deteriorate or improve. All hikes in this book are circuitous, and can be shortened or modified by referring to the maps. As a last resort, you can drive most of the hikes described in this book.

Urban Hikes

Downtown

Washington Monument and Mt. Vernon Square

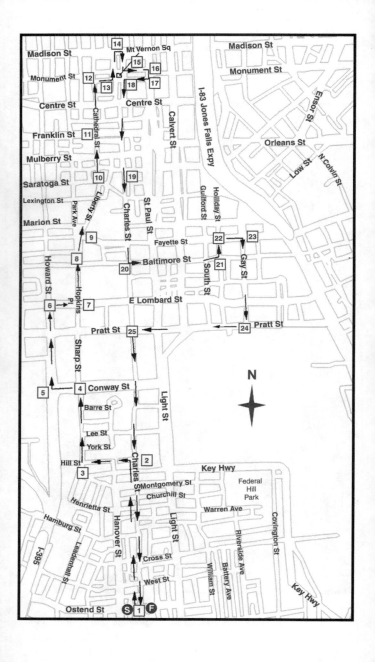

Overview

Distance: Four-and-one-half miles.

Major attractions: The neighborhoods of Federal Hill, Otterbein, and Mount Vernon; and the downtown business district destroyed by the great fire of 1904.

Starting location: The intersection of Charles and Ostend streets in the Federal Hill neighborhood.

Directions to start and parking: From downtown Baltimore, take St. Paul Street south, which becomes Light Street near the Inner Harbor. Continue on Light Street into South Baltimore. Two blocks past Cross Street Market, turn right onto Ostend Street. Continue on Ostend Street for one block, until it meets Charles Street. Free on-street parking is usually available around this intersection.

From the south, approach Baltimore on I-95. Take Exit 52, Russell Street. Continue north on Russell Street past the Resco generating plant and Raven Stadium. Just before Oriole Park at Camden Yards, follow signs for Hamburg Street. Turn right onto Hamburg Street. Continue on Hamburg Street for about one-half mile, until it dead-ends at Charles Street. Turn right onto Charles Street. Continue on Charles Street for three blocks, until it meets Ostend Street. Free on-street parking is usually available around this intersection.

Access to eating facilities: Charles Street hosts many restaurants, take-outs, and convenience stores in the Federal Hill and Mt. Vernon neighborhoods.

Introduction

Baltimore's most defining moment happened on a blustery February morning in the year 1904. A fire erupted in a dry-goods store on the business district's west side. The blaze could have been easily extinguished, but a stiff breeze sent wayward sparks airborne, igniting neighboring buildings. A series of exploding gasoline tanks rampantly spread the flames. Within hours, the entire downtown was ablaze in what became one of the most destructive conflagrations in our country's history. Firemen from as far away as Altoona, Pennsylvania, and Wilmington, Delaware, rushed to the scene. H.L. Mencken reported on the fire from Washington, D.C., where the red glow of flames was visible. Twenty-four hours later, little remained of downtown Baltimore. Fifteen hundred buildings were leveled, and scores more charred. Damage was estimated at $150 million—well over $3 billion in today's dollars. The city of Baltimore was reduced to a pile of smoldering stone and brick with thousands of businesses and homes gone. In the destruction, however, blossomed a miracle: No lives were lost.

Baltimore's cavalry of engineers and urban planners saw the catastrophe as an opportunity to revamp their city. They widened the streets and better planned public services. They called on top architects to rebuild downed buildings. What emerged from one of our nation's most calamitous events was one of the nation's most attractive cities. This hike will explore the district of Baltimore rebuilt from the 1904 fire, and also traverse several interesting downtown residential communities.

1

**Begin the hike at the intersection of Charles and Ostend
streets. Walk north on Charles Street toward
downtown Baltimore. Continue on Charles Street
for about one-half mile.**

This hike begins in the Federal Hill neighborhood,
which is among the most popular in the city. The recent
deluge of post-collegiate professionals has driven up real
estate prices, and resulted in the emergence of trendy cafés,
pubs, and shops—many of which flank South Charles Street.

Two of the most popular cafés in the neighborhood are
Mother's Federal Hill Grille and Vespas, located just before
Cross Street. These two cafés occupy what was once Muhly's
Bakery. This business establishment supplied South
Baltimore residents with breads and sweets from 1852
through the early 1990s. Eberhardt Muhly was a German
carpenter who built an oven in his backyard at 1115 South
Charles Street. He fueled it with scraps of wood left over
from his business. Besides baking his own bread, Muhly
allowed neighbors to bring their dough, which he would
bake for two pennies each. Five years later, Muhly laid down
his hammer for good, becoming a full-time baker. Across the
street, in the Provident Bank building, is Boomerang Pub, an
Australian restaurant.

Pay particular attention to the Caffé Brio, just before
Henrietta Street. Caffé Brio is one of Baltimore's favorite
coffee shops, and a great place to refresh after this hike. Its
vegetarian menu particularly endears it to local vegans.

The block of three-story brick residences between
Henrietta and Montgomery streets is the Montgomery
Square development. This development replaced a derelict
warehouse that stood for decades. The homes were built in
the early 1990s to meet the increased demand for housing in
Federal Hill. The Federal Hill Neighborhood Association
made sure they were designed in deference to the neighborhood's historic rowhouses. Across from the Montgomery
Square development is Scarborough Fair—Federal Hill's only
bed and breakfast.

Christ Lutheran Church stands just past Hughes Street. The tall white building peeking from behind the church is The Lutheran Center, which is the corporate headquarters of several offices of the Lutheran Church, including many with international appeal. The ground floor of The Lutheran Center contains the Global Village Market store, offering a variety of handicrafts made by artisans in emerging nations. Much of the profit from sale of the goods goes back to the impoverished artisans.

2

At Christ Lutheran Church, turn left onto Hill Street, which is partially laid in brick. Continue on Hill Street for two blocks.

This is the neighborhood of Otterbein, whose name has become synonymous with urban renewal. Otterbein, by virtue of its proximity to Baltimore's harbor, has played a vital role in the city's growth. But by the 1970s, it had degraded into the poster child for urban decay. Rowhouses were reduced to shells, many with collapsed roofs. Flophouses

---

What a Buck will Buy

Otterbein's rise from pestilence can be attributed to then-Mayor William Donald Schaefer and his cohort, Robert Emery, Jr., who was the city's housing commissioner. In 1975, the duo devised a revivification plan called "dollar housing." The premise was that vacant house shells would be sold to qualified buyers for the bargain basement price of one dollar, under the condition that the buyer fixed up the house to a level acceptable to the city, and in an appropriate time frame. More than 100 shells in Otterbein were placed on the market and 800 prospective buyers expressed interest at an open house, so a lottery was held to select the winners. To accommodate the rehabs, the city provided technical expertise and low-cost loans. Urban homesteaders invaded the streets of Otterbein with a vengeance, and within two years, the refurbished neighborhood sparkled, as it does today.

lined the streets, attracting crime and suspect visitors. Filth and rats abounded. In his book *Federal Hill*, Norman Rukert notes that this area was a mecca for gambling events, including spirited cockfights and pit bull brawls. Otterbein was essentially a dead neighborhood. An ingenious renewal program called "dollar housing" revived the moribund community, and today it is one of the most attractive and desirable in the city.

In one block, Hill Street crosses Hanover Street. Hanover Street temporarily dead-ends at the one-block-long public park to the right. At the end of the park is a large metal wheel laid on its side. This relic served as a turnstile for the city's public trolley system, which operated until the 1960s.

Cross Hanover Street and note the homes to the left, which are dollar houses. They show that with forethought and a plan, life can emerge from depravity. Hill Street and other residential byways in Otterbein are among the most beautiful in the city. The return on investment for homeowners under the dollar-housing program would make any financial planner envious; the typical Otterbein house now sells for over one-quarter million dollars. The former St. Veronica's Church, at 120 Hill Street, was converted to condominium units during the renewal.

3
Turn right onto Sharp Street.
Continue on Sharp Street for three blocks.

The towering elm tree across Sharp Street is known as the Douglass Elm. From beneath it, Frederick Douglass orated one of his many freedom speeches. Around this intersection was the home of the former Tepper Hotel, which, as late as the 1940s, was considered one of the finest brothels in town. Many business establishments in the former Otterbein relied heavily on the patronage of sailors visiting Baltimore's port.

In one block, Lee Street intersects to the right. Lee Street connects the heart of Otterbein with the waterfront. The lot at 123 West Lee Street once housed the St. Joseph's Roman Catholic Church, but was razed during the homesteading movement and replaced with three fill-in houses; 118 West Lee Street is where the priests once lived, and 125 West Lee Street where the nuns lived; 132 West Lee Street was constructed from remains of the Tepper Hotel. Most houses on Lee Street date to the nineteenth century, though 124 West Lee Street dates to 1792.

The popular Jos. A. Banks and Sons retail clothing shops, located throughout the Washington, D.C., and Baltimore areas, originated in a tailor shop on the southeast corner of Lee and Sharp streets. The former shop is now a private residence.

4

Cross over and turn left onto Conway Street. Continue on Conway Street for one block.

Just across Conway Street is the Old Otterbein Church, which lent the neighborhood its name. The church is the city's oldest, still in continuous use by its congregation. It remains undaunted by the extensive construction happening around it, which only seems to accentuate the church's simple beauty. The Old Otterbein Church was built in 1785 as a German Evangelical Reformed Church, and was constructed from the ballast of ships visiting the harbor. It was named for an early pastor, Philip Wilhelm Otterbein, whose grave is on the grounds. The original name of the sanctuary was the Old Otterbein United Methodist Church. To the left of the Old Otterbein Church is the Baltimore Convention Center.

Conway Street runs smack into the outer right field wall of Oriole Park at Camden Yards. Open for business in 1992, Oriole Park may be major league baseball's premier venue to take in a ball game. It has ushered in the profitable philosophy that a baseball game is not a one-dimensional event, but a multi-faceted spectacle. Snazzy diamond-vision screens light up the walls, and raucous music fills the seats between innings. Food and souvenir vendors work the alley behind the right field wall. The throwback aura of Oriole Park gives spectators a greater feeling of intimacy with action on the field.

This premise has been replicated in other big-league stadiums (Detroit, Cleveland, Texas). The Oriole Park structure is anchored by the former B&O Warehouse, which runs parallel to Howard Street, and, at over one-fifth of a mile long, is said to be the longest brick structure on the East Coast.

It was at Oriole Park that, in 1995, future Hall of Famer Cal Ripken, Jr., broke Lou Gehrig's streak by appearing in 2,131 consecutive ball games. Ripken may be Baltimore's most hallowed player, but the baseball afficionado recognizes the neighborhood of Oriole Park as home to a ballplayer of equal stature. Babe Ruth's birthplace was at 216 Emory Street, two blocks northwest of the stadium. It is now home to the Babe Ruth Museum. His father operated Ruth's Cafe, which was at 406 Conway Street, now the location of center field. A statue of The Babe is located just west of Oriole Park's Eutaw Street entrance, but only the staunchest ball fan will notice that Babe is grasping a right-hander's glove, when he was in fact a southpaw. (For a brief spell at St. Mary's Industrial School, young Babe Ruth did use a righthanded mitt because the school did not have lefthanded ones. He caught balls, dropped his glove, and threw with the same hand.)

5

Turn right onto I-395 (Howard Street), directly in front of Oriole Park at Camden Yards. Continue on Howard Street for two blocks.

Just past Oriole Park is the former Camden Station, which stands on the stadium's north parking lot. Camden Station was once the primary rail entry into downtown Baltimore. Directly behind the station, a massive shed structure once spread out along what is now Howard Street, accommodating incoming trains. The tracks extended outward toward what is now I-95. Camden Station is where Abraham Lincoln's body arrived in Baltimore following his assassination at Ford's Theatre in Washington, D.C.

Near Camden Station, the Bromo-Seltzer Tower comes into view. This is one of Baltimore's most endearing and enduring landmarks. The tower is a 288-foot-high replication of the Palazzo Vecchio in Florence, Italy. It was made to be the headquarters of the Emerson Drug Company, which sold Bromo-Seltzer in its trademark cobalt-blue bottles. When the Bromo-Seltzer Tower opened in 1911, a fifty-one-foot-high reproduction of a cobalt Bromo-Seltzer bottle rotated on its roof, reflecting a blue beam visible from Maryland's eastern shore. Almost 600 light bulbs illuminated the beam. The bottle was removed in 1936 for safety reasons; it wobbled dangerously in high winds. The Emerson Drug Company eventually moved away, and the Bromo-Seltzer Tower is now officially titled the Baltimore Arts Tower. Plans are in place to convert it to high-rent apartments. Notice that letters of the word Bromo-Seltzer serve as numbers on the clock.

6

Turn right onto Lombard Street.
Continue on Lombard Street for one block.

The 1st Mariner Arena is situated just past Lombard Street. The arena was home to the Baltimore Bullets, who in the early 1970s packed pro basketball's most potent one-two punch with Wes Unseld and Elvin Hayes. It's now home of the Baltimore Blast professional soccer team. An assortment of productions are also held here, including the Ice Capades, concerts, professional wrestling, and monster truck rallies. The arena is Baltimore's largest indoor entertainment venue, providing seating for about 11,000 spectators. On September 13, 1964, the Beatles made their only Baltimore appearance at the arena, then known as the Civic Center.

An event of immense historical significance occurred on the grounds now occupied by the 1st Mariner Arena. The year was 1776, and the British were pushing on Philadelphia, which was then capital of the United States. The Continental Congress, composed of the era's most important statesmen (including future president John Adams), fled the city fearing capture. They agreed to regroup in Baltimore, at its largest structure, which was an important social hall where the arena now stands. There, they voted to give General George Washington absolute power to lead the fight against the British. The social hall came to be called Congress Hall.

7

Turn left onto Hopkins Place. Continue on Hopkins Place.

The 1st Mariner Arena supplanted one of Baltimore's most vibrant shopping districts. Historical photographs of Hopkins Place show hurried shoppers by the hundreds rushing from store to store, and vendors hawking anything imaginable. This section of old Baltimore was reminiscent of Broadway in Manhattan. Howard Street, which runs parallel to and one block west of Hopkins Place, was the main thoroughfare of this neighborhood's shopping district, and remains a busy shopping district for Baltimore's African-American community. It is being targeted for a possible large-scale urban renewal project.

Along the east side of the 1st Mariner Arena was the epicenter of the great fire of 1904. It started in a six-story dry-goods building owned by John E. Hurst and Company. The store was located on German Street, which was later renamed Redwood Street. The fire's decimation extended to Jones Falls to the east, Fayette Street to the north, Hopkins Place to the west, and the Inner Harbor to the south.

8

Cross over Baltimore Street. Hopkins Place becomes Liberty Street. Continue on Liberty Street.

9

One block past Baltimore Street, Liberty Street forks to the right, and Park Avenue continues straight ahead. Fork right onto Liberty Street.

The cream-colored building at 20 Park Avenue, on the southwest corner of Park Avenue and Fayette Street, was constructed in 1896 in an architectural style known as Beaux-Arts. Beaux-Arts was popular in Paris at the time, and features symmetrical facades with lots of repetitive ornamentation and recesses; 20 Park Avenue today houses attorney offices.

The Baltimore Gas and Electric Building is located on Liberty Street just before Lexington Street. BGE was formed in 1816, and became the first utility in the nation to distribute gas and one of the first to distribute electricity. Such a venerable operation commanded a commensurate headquarters. Spin around to see the ornate bronze and marble facade, which faces a pedestrian walkway on what was once Lexington Street. The four eight-foot figures in bas-relief on the fourth floor's exterior respectively represent knowledge, light, heat, and power. Near the entry, notice the bronze statue of a horse bursting from a concrete block.

Cross Lexington Street, and look left. Lexington Street becomes a pedestrian shopping strip for the next two blocks, terminating at Lexington Market. The market is the granddaddy of Baltimore's neighborhood farmers' markets, and features over one hundred stalls of food, flowers, and other wares. A market has stood at this location since 1782, but the present structure was built soon after a fire leveled the then-existing shed building in 1949. Lexington Market over the decades has been a showcase for ethnic foods, reflecting the waves of immigrants that swept over Baltimore. It's said that George Washington and Thomas Jefferson visited here. The two-block pedestrian shopping strip leading to Lexington Market was opened in 1974 as a way to provide conveniences to city dwellers in hopes of preventing urban flight.

The parking lot to the right, just before Saratoga Street, is former site of the elegant Rennert Hotel. Built in 1885, the Rennert Hotel was among the most popular in town, thanks to its location in the heart of the bustling shopping district. But like so many other lodging and dining establishments, the Rennert Hotel could not survive the blow dealt by Prohibition, and was forced to close. It was razed in 1941 to make room for a five-story parking garage, which was leveled in 1996.

10
Cross over Saratoga Street.
Liberty Street becomes Cathedral Street.

Across Saratoga Street, Liberty Street becomes Cathedral Street. The brick house at Saratoga Street is the Old St. Paul's Church Rectory, where the church's rectors used to live. The church is the brick structure visible east on Saratoga Street. The Old St. Paul's Church Rectory is a modified Federal-style house, with a detailed Palladian window above the entrance. The house is only one room deep—typical of Federal design of the era. Today, it is appropriately the head-quarters of Preservation Maryland, which is the state's oldest historic preservation organization. As you pass the rectory, notice the terra cotta inlays in the brickwork.

The white rowhouse on the right side of Saratoga Street looking west is Marconi's restaurant, which is among Baltimore's most venerable eating establishments. Through the years it has maintained an old-world charm and unpre-tentiousness, which might be the reason it was one of H.L. Mencken's favorite haunts. It's been rumored that Rudolf Valentino lived upstairs and served as waiter here prior to becoming an actor.

The Enoch Pratt Free Library stands just past Mulberry Street. Enoch Pratt was a Massachusetts philanthropist who settled in Baltimore around 1831. He made his money in hardware and iron. In 1882, Pratt gave Baltimore the gift of books, providing the funding for several library buildings, including one at this location. These were among the first public libraries in the country. Interestingly, Pratt was not a reader, but came from New England, where books were engrained in the culture. The present library is the headquar-ters of the Enoch Pratt system, and was erected in 1933. The library contains rooms dedicated to H.L. Mencken and Edgar Allan Poe. The Mencken Room opens to the public one day each year—on September 12th to honor the sage's birthday. Of particular architectural interest is the unassum-ing front facade and entrance. Whereas most libraries built at the time featured grand entrances with columns and dramatic stairways, designers instead chose to keep this entrance simple and at street level. This was to facilitate public viewing of the display windows located along Cathedral Street.

Immediately across from the Enoch Pratt Free Library is the Basilica of the National Shrine of the Assumption of the Blessed Virgin Mary, also known as the Baltimore Cathedral. The country's oldest cathedral, it is known as the Mother Church of Roman Catholicism in the United States. Architectural historian Nikolaus Pevsner called it "North America's most beautiful building." The Basilica was designed by Benjamin Latrobe, and dedicated in 1821. Latrobe also designed the United States Capitol Building, but the Basilica is considered his masterpiece. Latrobe never saw completion of his prize, as he died one year before its dedication. The Basilica, as envisioned and designed by Latrobe, was built on the area's highest point and could be prominently seen from all directions, including the city's waterfront. Now it is swallowed by neighboring buildings. A quick peek into the Basilica is recommended if the doors are open.

Next to the Basilica is the soup kitchen Our Daily Bread, operated by Associated Catholic Charities. Our Daily Bread serves close to one thousand patrons each day—the most famous being Pope John Paul II, who ate here during his 1995 visit to Baltimore. Our Daily Bread is embroiled in the city's controversial plan to relocate all its individual homeless facilities to one large "homeless campus" away from downtown. Some shop and restaurant owners along Charles Street complained that the congestion of homeless people around Our Daily Bread's building deters business.

11

Continue on Cathedral Street past Franklin Street.

The tall green-trimmed building across from the Bread of Life at the Cathedral Church, in the former YMCA building, is the Mt. Vernon Hotel. The hotel is affiliated with the

Baltimore International College, which is the parent organization of the Baltimore Culinary College. The seventh and eighth floors of the Mt. Vernon Hotel serve as dormitories for the Baltimore International College. In the past, the hotel has served as a training ground for students in the college.

The Clarion Hotel stands at the corner of Cathedral and Monument streets, facing Mt. Vernon Square park. This was formerly the Peabody Court Hotel. A conservatory restaurant on the top floor, though not visible from street level, offers panoramic views of the city and is a popular wedding reception spot.

12

In front of the Clarion Hotel, turn right onto West Mt. Vernon Place (Monument Street). Continue on West Mt. Vernon Place for one block.

Before turning, look north on Cathedral Street. Both 702 and 704 Cathedral Street are houses of historical significance. The brick and stone house at 702 Cathedral Street was the home of businessman William J. Albert. Abraham Lincoln was the overnight guest of Albert here on April 18, 1864. Lincoln was in town to speak at the Maryland Institute, at that time located around the harbor. Afterwards, he met with abolitionists here. The brownstone next door, 704 Cathedral Street, was home to H.L. Mencken and his wife Sara immediately following their wedding. Sara died of tuberculosis five years later, and Mencken moved back into his childhood rowhouse on Hollins Street in West Baltimore.

West Mt. Vernon Place cuts through Mt. Vernon Square, where many of Baltimore's elite settled over a century ago. Back then, Mt. Vernon Square was the pulsing heart of Baltimore City. To call the square upscale would have been an understatement; it was among the wealthiest blocks in the nation. Mt. Vernon Square has physically changed little over time; the array of fountains and statues still accent the park, and stately mansions still frame the square. However, many of the wealthy have fled, and most of the former residences have been subdivided into condominiums, office space, or prestigious clubs. Frank R. Shivers, Jr., in *Walking in Baltimore: An Intimate Guide to the Old City*, said of Mt. Vernon Square: "Probably nowhere else in America can you still see so clearly the lost world of the big-city rich at their apogee." Mt. Vernon Square is home to several of Baltimore's most enjoyable outdoor fairs, including the flower festival in spring and literary festival in autumn.

The Garrett-Jacobs House stands at 7-11 West Mt. Vernon Place. It's presently home to the Engineering Society of Baltimore, which formed just after the great fire to plan the city's reconstruction. The Garrett-Jacobs House was formerly a residence—the largest and most costly in the city. B&O Railroad magnate John Work Garrett purchased a very traditional rowhouse on the site for his son and stepdaughter, Robert and Mary Frick Garrett. It was thought to have been built around 1853. Over the next forty years, Mary Frick turned it into the consummate residential showpiece, partly by annexing three adjacent houses. Her final dwelling boasted over forty rooms, including a theater. A Tiffany stained-glass window above a carved wooden stairway is the house's crown jewel. Hollywood location scouts are well aware of the Garrett-Jacobs House's allure; scenes from *The Accidental Tourist*, *Her Alibi*, *Diner*, and *Twelve Monkeys* were filmed here.

Renovation of the Garrett-Jacobs House was not without controversy. At one point, Mary Frick Jacobs (now remarried to Dr. Henry Jacobs following the death of her first husband) brownstoned the facade and extended the entrance with a vestibule. Harry Janes, owner of an adjacent house, complained that the "monstrous vestibule" cut off his view of the Washington Monument and did not complement the more conservative houses that lined the square. A lengthy court battle ensued, in which the Jacobses ultimately emerged victorious. To celebrate, they bought the Janes's house and razed the back portion of it to allow more light into their stairwell.

Notice the interesting carved doors on 3 and 5 West Mt. Vernon Place. To historians, 1 West Mt. Vernon Place is known as the Thomas-Jencks-Gladding House, named after the families that lived here. It played host to such luminaries as Warren Harding, Mrs. Herbert Hoover, and the former Prince of Wales (Queen Victoria's son) who later became King Edward VII of England. To art lovers, however, 1 West Mt. Vernon Place is the Hackerman House, the most recent addition to the Walters Art Museum, and home to its extensive Asian arts collection.

The homes on the north side of West Mt. Vernon Place are equally impressive. The wide white dwelling at 8 West Mt. Vernon Place is the Tiffany-Fisher-Randall House. Built in 1842, it's the oldest building on Mt. Vernon Square, and once hosted the Duke and Duchess of Windsor for an overnight stay. The dwelling is now home to the Mt. Vernon Club, a private women's organization.

The 178-foot-tall Washington Monument stands at the bull's-eye of Mount Vernon Square. It was completed in 1829 (after taking fourteen years to build) as the first monument in the country to commemorate George Washington. The original intent was to place the Washington Monument in the center of downtown Baltimore, but too many people feared what would happen if it tumbled. It was instead erected on a barren hill overlooking town, where the monument could be seen from below, but do no damage if toppled. Upper class members of society began building their homes around the beautiful monument, and the location became Mt. Vernon Square. Robert Mills designed the column of the Washington Monument, which was built of marble, mined in Cockeysville. Mills later designed the District of Columbia's Washington Monument on which work started five years after this one was completed (construction of the D.C. monument took only fifty years to complete). Enrico Causici carved the sixteen-foot statue on top of the Baltimore monument, which depicts Washington submitting his resignation as commander-in-chief of the Continental Army. Those who clamber the monument's 228 steps are rewarded with stunning views of Baltimore.

13

Turn left onto the west side of Washington Place (Charles Street). Continue on Washington Place for one block.

A Beaux-Arts apartment building stands at 700 Washington Place. Built in 1906, this building brings European flair to the square. Apartment living was in great demand a century ago, and people sometimes spent decades on waiting lists.

Next to this building is the Stafford Hotel. At one time this hotel was Baltimore's lap of luxury. Many wealthy Baltimoreans wintered here to escape their unheated homes. F. Scott Fitzgerald once took residence here. The American Psychoanalytic Association formed in the Stafford Hotel in 1911. Today, the Stafford Hotel is used as subsidized housing. The French chateau adjacent to the Stafford Hotel is the Graham-Hughes House. Its ostentation may seem out of place in the conservative Mt. Vernon Square, but it was a design popular with the upper class at the time of its construction in 1895. Charles Cassell showed his architectural range by designing both the Stafford Hotel and the Graham-Hughes House.

14

Walk around the statue of John Eager Howard and head directly back on the east side of Washington Place. Continue on Washington Place for one block.

Mt. Vernon Square was built on John Eager Howard's former estate, which spanned seven hundred acres. Howard's estate home was a magnificent Georgian mansion with sweeping views of the harbor. He called it "Belvedere," meaning "beautiful view." Look for the tall red-bricked building with mansard roof perched about four blocks north on Charles Street. This is the Belvedere Hotel, built on the site of Howard's former mansion. The Belvedere was Baltimore's preeminent hotel from its construction in 1903 through the 1950s, when entertainers and jet-setters frequented its many bars and tea rooms. The fortunes of the Belvedere suddenly plummeted, and by the 1970s its role was limited to that of college dormitory. The Belvedere has since been renovated into condominiums, and is still home to the famous Owl Bar, which was one of Baltimore's most popular speakeasies during Prohibition.

Baltimore is home to a number of obscure, but interesting, museums. One is the Mt. Vernon Museum of Incandescent Lighting, located at 717 Washington Place. The museum was the obsessive by-product of a dentist, Dr. Hugh Francis Hicks, now deceased, whose main source of pride was his collection of 60,000 light bulbs. The display, to date housed in the basement of his dentistry practice, is temporarily closed as it awaits a move to one or more other local museums.

The green-tinted Mt. Vernon Methodist Church stands beside the Washington Monument. Most churches built in the late nineteenth century were designed in the Gothic style, and this one teeters on the downright macabre. It was built out of locally quarried green serpentine marble and red sandstone, rocks that do not wear well. The church's sheen has darkened over time and stones occasionally require replacement. Major cosmetic surgery was done in 1932 and 1978. Flowers, vines, creatures, and other nature icons embellish its facade. The church was designed by Thomas Dixon, who is also responsible for the Dixon Hill development in Mt. Washington. In 1843, Francis Scott Key died in a house formerly located on this site.

15

Turn left at the Mt. Vernon Methodist Church onto East Mt. Vernon Place. Continue on East Mt. Vernon Place for one block.

At 10 East Mt. Vernon Place is the Asbury House, which is owned by the Mt. Vernon Methodist Church. Though it was built in 1855, the attractive facade was not added until a renovation in the 1890s. It is the former home of a prosperous German merchant. Just ahead, at 22 through 32 East Mt. Vernon Place, known as Brownstone Row, are Baltimore's finest examples of brownstone buildings, evocative of turn-of-the-last-century Manhattan. The buildings today have been carved into office space and condominiums. Notice the boot cleaner at 24 East Mt. Vernon Place, at the base of the front stairs.

16
Turn right onto St. Paul Street.
Continue on St. Paul Street for about one hundred feet.

17
Turn right onto the south side of East Mt. Vernon Place.
Continue on East Mt. Vernon Place for one block.

The buildings to the left comprise the Peabody Institute. Established in 1857 by local philanthropist George Peabody, it was the first institution in the country dedicated to the education of professional musicians and it remains one of the most prestigious. After a period of financial difficulties, the institute fell under the auspices of Johns Hopkins University in 1977. The list of musicians who either studied or performed at the Peabody reads like a "Who's Who in American Music."

The library of the Peabody Institute may be Baltimore's most precious example of art, space, and design. From an architectural perspective, it's considered one of the finest interiors in the city. The main reading room is of open design, with a high ceiling and a marble floor dramatically laid with black and white diamond-shaped tiles. Encircling it are six levels of balconies, each enclosed with an ornate wrought-iron handrail. The room is capped with an expansive skylight. The library has been called a "Cathedral of Books." H.L. Mencken reserved a private table here while researching and writing his notable tome, *The American Language*.

18

Turn left onto Washington Place (Charles Street). Continue on Charles Street toward the harbor.

The white-washed Schapiro House stands at 609 Washington Place. The cast-iron grillwork embellishing its balconies was popular in Baltimore generations ago. Much of Baltimore's cast iron has been stripped off the houses and donated to scrap metal drives during various wars. Today, the Schapiro House serves as an office building for the Peabody Institute.

Directly across from the Schapiro House is the Walters Art Museum, which began as one of the largest private art collections in the world. It grew from the personal collection of William Walters, who made his money in liquor and the railroad. Walters had a penchant for the works of local artists, and amassed an impressive collection. During the Civil War, he fled to Europe and cultivated new tastes. Walters returned to his Mt. Vernon home in 1874 with a greatly expanded collection, and allowed visitors to view it for a fee, which he donated to charity. After Walters died in 1894, his son Henry continued collecting and showcasing the family's pride, but needed more space. He opened what is now the main building of the Walters Art Museum in 1909 for that purpose. Its interior design replicates the University Center at the University of Genoa. Upon his death, Henry bequeathed the collection to the city, and the museum has undergone several major expansions.

At 516 North Charles Street is A People United, a store that sells goods made by women in third-world countries. Like the Global Village Market store in Federal Hill, it provides an extra dash of financial support to the artisans.

The bold white church on the northwest corner of Charles and Franklin streets is the First Unitarian Church. It was built in 1818 and is the country's oldest Unitarian church building still in use. Its basic design is a dome capping a cube. Some think Unitarians are religious rebels, but in reality they are an educated, free-thinking sect not bound by a single creed or denomination. They are united by the belief in one God, and by their belief in human equality and community service. Enoch Pratt and George Peabody were two prominent members of the local Unitarian Church. The national organization has also attracted such independent thinkers as Thomas Jefferson and Ralph Waldo Emerson.

The First Unitarian Church recently received a needed facelift. Notice the terra-cotta relief "Angel of Truth" above the Franklin Street entrance. It's a 1950s replica of the original figure that had deteriorated. Soon after the church's completion, the congregation realized that the plaster dome ceiling of the sanctuary created poor acoustics. A false ceiling was installed to contain the sound. Slaves of the church members were known to sit in pews hidden in the church.

Just past the First Unitarian Church, behind the Basilca on Cathedral Street, is the Archbishop of Baltimore's residence at 408 North Charles Street. Dating to 1829, this is where Cardinal Gibbons lived for about fifty years. For twenty-five of those years, he served as the only American Cardinal. It's currently the home of Cardinal William H. Keeler. Notice the stone marker just past the house commemorating a special tree in the yard.

Upton Sinclair, author of *The Jungle*, once lived at 415 North Charles Street, which is now home to the American Heart Association. This stretch of Charles Street also contains interesting restaurants ranging from fine dining to inexpensive ethnic food. Sotto Sopra, at 405 North Charles Street, is an attractive special-occasion eatery featuring Italian cuisine. Across the street, look for Thai, Ethiopian, Japanese, Afghan, and Irish eateries. This section of Charles Street started out as primarily a residential street with few businesses. Following the fire of 1904, businesses were forced to move from the downtown area during reconstruction, and many settled along this stretch of Charles Street. In 1915, the Charles Street Association was formed to fight this transformation. It was Baltimore's first formal neighborhood organization.

Both 343 and 345 North Charles Street have attractive marble facades. These were installed in the 1920s when many

Charles Street merchants found it fashionable to add such embellishments. The Woman's Industrial Exchange is at 333 North Charles Street. This institution began just after the Civil War, and allowed impoverished women—many of them widows—to support themselves by selling handcrafted items such as quilts and needlework. A dining room was added later, and still operates today. There were once seventy-two such Woman's Industrial Exchanges in the nation. Baltimore's branch is the oldest of those remaining. Meg Ryan and Rosie O'Donnell can be seen dining at this Woman's Industrial Exchange in the movie *Sleepless in Seattle*.

Brown's Arcade stands at 326 North Charles Street and consists of a group of 1820s rowhouses that were transformed into businesses. They were named for Governor Frank Brown, who assisted the architect in the conversion. Downs Stationery, at 317 North Charles Street, is the only existing business along the North Charles Street corridor that opened its doors before World War II. It was the social center of the Mt. Vernon bourgeois, and where the all-important debutante list and social calendar were kept.

The old YMCA building, built in 1873, is the triangular structure at the crossing of Charles and Saratoga streets. Although it maintains a fine mansard roof and dormers, the original building included towers and turrets. It was Baltimore city's first YMCA.

19
Continue on Charles Street past Saratoga Street.

Across Saratoga Street begins the part of Baltimore destroyed by the fire. The Old St. Paul's Episcopal Church to the left, however, escaped the burn. It has the distinction of being the only property in Baltimore City that has remained under the same ownership since the original survey of the city was completed in 1730. The present building is the fourth structure on the site, and was completed in 1856. The design is of an Italian Romanesque basilica, and a planned steeple tower was never completed. The facade is highlighted by a triple-arched portico, and two bas-relief stone carvings—one of Christ and the other of Moses.

The seven-story Masonic Temple stands at 223 through 227 North Charles Street. It was built in 1869, and renovated just after the great fire. Masons are a charitable and civic organization. This particular temple contains several large and attractive meeting rooms, and in 1997 was sold to owners of the nearby Tremont Hotel to be used for banquet facilities.

At 217 North Charles Street is the headquarters of the Downtown Partnership of Baltimore, which is a non-profit organization dedicated to making downtown Baltimore City a great place to "invest, work, live, and play." Although the organization involves itself in beautification projects and setting public policy, their most visible role involves the many employees, clad in red and purple, who walk the downtown streets assisting tourists and locals.

The Fidelity Building, built in 1893, stands at the northwest corner of Lexington and Charles streets, immediately across from the Downtown Partnership headquarters. The first eight floors of this building are solid granite, and the floors above it are steel-framed, with terra-cotta facings to match the granite. The Central Savings Bank stands cater-corner, on the southeast corner of that intersection. These two buildings were among the few to survive the great fire.

The striking skyscraper with smoky glass standing next to the Fidelity Building is known as One Charles Center. It was designed by the world-renowned architect Ludwig Mies van der Rohe, and built in 1962. Rohe's signature office buildings feature stark, unadorned facades and forms. One Charles Center was immediately lauded as a masterpiece by both the city and critics. It stands on the site of the former O'Neill's department store. During the great fire, the owner of the department store fled to the Basilica of the Assumption, and prayed that if his building was spared, he would erect a cathedral somewhere in the city. It was, and upon his death, O'Neill left $8 million for construction of the spectacular Cathedral of Mary Our Queen, located on Charles Street in northern Baltimore City. That cathedral is viewable on the Roland Park Hike.

The Blaustein Building is the modern high-rise at the southeast corner of Fayette and Charles streets. It is named for the Blaustein family, who made their money in the oil industry. Russian-Jewish immigrant Louis Blaustein and his son Jacob began the family business by selling oil from the back of horse-drawn carts in the early 1900s. To make a long story short, that business became Amoco. The Blaustein Building opened in 1964 as the headquarters of the Crown Central Oil and American Trading and Production Company.

This part of downtown Baltimore is known as Charles Center, which is the result of a wholesale urban renewal project that started in the 1950s. City officials hoped to revivify the stagnant economy of downtown Baltimore by bulldozing thirty-three acres of buildings and replacing them with contemporary high-rises. Based on the revived economy that resulted, the venture was deemed a success, and the city was applauded for its innovative scheme. The Charles Center project extended toward the Inner Harbor, and paved the way for substantial renovation that occurred later around the waterfront. Several skywalks were included in the Charles Center renovation plan, but critics have maligned them as alienating street life, which they say is the core of the urban experience.

The intersection of Baltimore and Charles streets marks Baltimore's ground zero, the separation point for the city's four quadrants. The Baltimore and Ohio Railroad Building occupies the intersection's northwest corner. The building's lobby is a showpiece of Italian marble and leaded glass, and well worth a visit. The original B&O Building was destroyed in the 1904 fire.

The striking Morris A. Mechanic Theatre stands across Baltimore Street from the B&O Railroad Building. To some, it's a masterpiece of form and function—perfect for a theatrical venue. To others, it's a concrete eyesore. It was described by its architect John M. Johansen as being "functional expressionism." The 1,600-seat Mechanic Theatre features Broadway productions, and debuted in 1967 with a showing of *Hello Dolly* starring Betty Grable. The theater is ironically named for Morris Abel Mechanic, a Baltimore developer who gained a reputation for razing old theaters and replacing them with more profitable ventures. This intersection was once called Sun Square, named for the Baltimore Sun Building, which formerly stood where the Mechanic Theatre stands today.

20

Turn left onto Baltimore Street.
Continue on Baltimore Street for three blocks.

The former bank building on the southeast corner of Baltimore and Charles streets resembles the Erechtheum on the Acropolis in Athens. Four massive Ionic columns line Baltimore Street, and six lesser columns stretch along Charles Street. The ornamentation along the base of the columns, and the lion heads along the cornices of the building, were molded from casts that came from Athens.

Just before Light Street and to the right is the Bank of America Center. This building has the gilded gold roof that splashes sunshine across the city when viewed from a distance. At thirty-four stories and 780 feet tall, it was the tallest building in the city when it opened in 1929 as the Baltimore Trust Building. It may be the finest example of large-scale Art Deco in the city. Cross Light Street and look left for a view of the Baltimore courthouse.

Just before Calvert Street to the right is the Chevy Chase Bank. In 1900, this building housed the Alex Brown Investment Banking Company, which is America's oldest investment and banking house in continuous operation. The Chevy Chase Bank building withstood the great fire of 1904, and is the only building in the city that displays visible damage from that fire. Look for rock chipping and scarring on the stone above the doorway and elsewhere around the structure. Temperatures at this location during the fire were estimated at 2,500 degrees Fahrenheit. The building escaped total devastation because it was surrounded by taller buildings, which created an updraft, causing the flames to leapfrog over it.

Cross Calvert Street, and look left. One block up is the Battle Monument. This statue punctuates Monument

Square, and commemorates the defeat of the British in 1814. This unique monument of Egyptian design was created by Parisian Maximilian Godefroy, who replicated a design popular in France in the early nineteenth century. Monument Square is flanked by Baltimore's courthouse facilities.

Just beyond Calvert Street, the stretch of businesses to the right represents one of the most architecturally interesting spots in the city. Notice the eclectic designs and uneven roofline. The green-faced building at the end of the row, at 231 East Baltimore Street, contained the offices of the *News American*, one of the city's former newspapers. The Sun Iron Building once stood at this site, and may have been Baltimore's most significant offering to the architectural community. It was the first commercial cast-iron-front building in the country, and likely the world. The Sun Iron Building was essentially the precursor to the modern-day skyscraper. It was headquarters of *The Sun* for over fifty years, but succumbed to the great fire in 1904. The success of this building, however, spawned a spate of similar iron buidings across the country.

21
Turn left onto Holliday Street (Commerce Street is to the right). Continue on Holliday Street for one block.

Baltimore Street, between Holliday and Gay streets, is a sordid clutch of strip bars and porn shops known as "The Block." The Block once spread across several blocks, and was Baltimore's famous red-light district, home to top-flight burlesque and vaudeville. Strippers such as Blaze Starr and Gypsy Rose Lee doffed their clothes here, and entertainers such as Jackie Gleason, Red Skelton, and Milton Berle performed to huge audiences. Over the past three decades, The Block has been reduced to a one-block stretch of strip joints and X-rated movie houses. Since The Block occupies prime center-city real estate, pressure from developers—not to mention competition from cable television and the Internet—will likely push it further toward extinction.

The Gayety Building stands just past Holliday Street to the right. The attractive facade of the Gayety Building pays tribute to a time when The Block was synonymous with a more classy variety of adult entertainment.

22

Turn right onto Fayette Street.
Continue on Fayette Street for one block.

City Hall stands on Holliday Street, just past Fayette Street. It was built in 1875 of French Baroque Revival design. Plans were in place to raze City Hall in 1975, citing the lack of adequate office space it provided. Then-Mayor William Donald Schaefer intervened with the decision to rehabilitate it instead. Two new floors were infilled to the four existing floors, in effect making six floors out of four. The iron roof is believed to be the largest of its kind.

The courtyard in front of City Hall is the War Memorial Plaza, where city events and rallies are staged. The namesake War Memorial stands at the east end of the plaza. The

---

Baltimore's Canyonland

The Legg Mason tower, located at 100 Light Street, is visible from throughout Baltimore's downtown district. It's identifiable by the name scrolled across its upper floor. Keep an eye peeled for a pair of large birds circling this office building. The thirty-third floor ledge of the Legg Mason building is home to a nesting pair of peregrine falcons. Until recently peregrine falcons were listed as "endangered" by the U.S. Fish and Wildlife Service. There are only 1,600 nesting pairs remaining in the United States and Canada. Peregrine falcons prefer to nest in steep, rugged canyons, which are simulated nicely by the skyscrapers of center cities. Nesting pairs can also be found in Pittsburgh, Cincinnati, Omaha, Harrisburg, and Montreal. This particular roost is ruled by a male named Beauregard, who has resided here since 1983. Beauregard has sired scores of offspring from his ledge, some of which have shown up in Dayton, Ohio, and Albany, New York.

impressive Greek Revival memorial was built in 1925 as a tribute to Marylanders who lost their lives in World War I. The memorial was rededicated in 1977 to include Marylanders killed in World War II, the Korean War, and the Vietnam War as well. Inside are displays of flags, firearms, uniforms, and other military relics. The horses flanking the War Memorial signify the Marine Corps.

23

Turn right onto Gay Street. Continue on Gay Street for four blocks, until it dead-ends on Pratt Street.

The United States Custom House stands at 40 South Gay Street, just before Lombard Street. This was where thousands of immigrants entering Baltimore's port over the past century were processed. The Custom House's interior walls are coated with numerous attractive murals, which have been called the finest decorative art collection in any public building in the country. Particularly noteworthy is the Call Room, where ship captains once conducted their business. A 1,800-square-foot mural of a maritime fleet graces its ceiling, and several others cover its walls—all painted by Francis Davis Millet. Just inside the Custom House's main entrance is a series of five murals, each depicting a significant historical vessel. The middle mural is of the *Mauritania*, the ship on which Millet lost his life when it sank on its maiden voyage. The Custom House stands on the site of the former domed Merchant's Exchange, which was demolished in 1900. The Merchant's Exchange building was where Abraham Lincoln lay in state awaiting burial.

Across Gay Street from the Custom House is the Holocaust Memorial. The dramatic statue along Lombard Street depicts people being swallowed by flames, and the rear concrete wall symbolizes a string of box cars—the sort that carried hundreds of thousands of European Jews to their death. The chilling words on the wall are from a survivor of Auschwitz. The memorial was dedicated in 1997 by the Baltimore Jewish Council, and replaced an earlier memorial at this location.

24

Turn right onto Pratt Street. Continue on Pratt Street for five blocks. Alternatively, walk along the Inner Harbor promenade paralleling Pratt Street.

Baltimore's Inner Harbor is one of the most popular tourist attractions in the country. For detailed descriptions of the attractions around the harbor see the Waterfront Hike.

25

Turn left onto Charles Street. Continue on Charles Street for just over one-half mile. This hike ends at the intersection of Charles and Ostend streets.

Suggested Reading

Books

Wish You Were Here! A Guide to Baltimore City for Natives and Newcomers by Carolyn Males, Carol Barbier Rolnick, and Pam Makowski Goresh

A Guide to Baltimore Architecture by John Dorsey and James D. Dilts

Walking in Baltimore: An Intimate Guide to the Old City by Frank R. Shivers, Jr.

Baltimore: The Building of an American City by Sherry H. Olson

Baltimore Transitions by Mark Miller

Websites

Baltimore City Government
www.ci.baltimore.md.us

Live Baltimore Home Center
www.livebaltimore.com

Downtown Partnership of Baltimore
www.godowntownbaltimore.com

Baltimore Area Convention and Visitors Association
www.baltconvstr.com

Welcome to South Baltimore
www.southbaltimore.com

Oriole Park at Camden Yards
www.ballparks.com/baseball/american/oriole.htm

Waterfront

USS *Constellation* at Inner Harbor

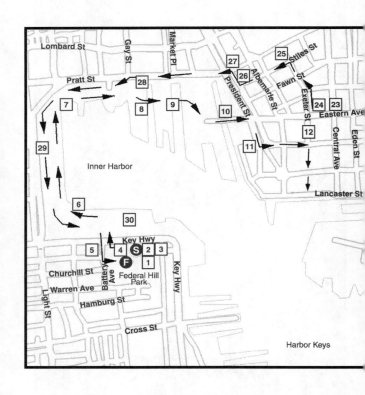

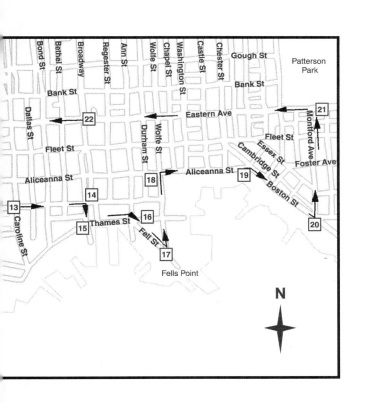

Bond St

Bethel St

Broadway

Regester St

Ann St

Wolfe St

Chapel St

Washington St

Castle St

Chester St

Gough St

Patterson Park

Bank St

Bank St

Eastern Ave

Dallas St

Fleet St

Aliceanna St

Caroline St

Durham St

Wolfe St

Aliceanna St

Fleet St

Montford Ave

21

Essex St

Cambridge St

Foster Ave

Boston St

13

14

18

19

20

15

Thames St

16

Fell St

17

Fells Point

N

Overview

Distance: Five-and-one-half miles.

Major attractions: The neighborhoods of Federal Hill, Fells Point, and Little Italy; and the Inner Harbor attractions.

Starting location: Federal Hill Park, located atop Federal Hill, which is adjacent to and south of Baltimore's Inner Harbor.

Directions to start and parking: From I-95, take I-395 toward downtown Baltimore. Follow signs for downtown and Inner Harbor attractions. Immediately in front of Oriole Park at Camden Yards, turn right onto Conway Street. Continue on Conway Street for four blocks until it dead-ends on the waterfront. Turn right onto Light Street, and move to the left lane. Continue on Light Street for two blocks, and veer left onto Key Highway, following the waterfront. Federal Hill Park is located to the right.

There are many parking lots and parking garages located around the Inner Harbor. An alternative is the long-term meter parking along Covington Street, just behind the American Visionary Art Museum. To get there, follow the directions above to Federal Hill. Just past the hill, turn right onto Covington Street and proceed for about one block. The meters are on the right. The long-term meters (ten-hour limit) are located farther up Covington Street than the short-term meters. Federal Hill Park can be easily accessed from its south side, away from the waterfront.

Access to eating facilities: The Inner Harbor, Little Italy, and Fells Point are rich in restaurants, pubs, and convenience stores.

Introduction

During his 1608 exploration of the Chesapeake Bay, Captain John Smith happened upon an interesting geologic protrusion of great color and form, which he described in his journal as "a great red bank of clay flanking a natural harbour basin." That day, Smith made the earliest record of what is now Federal Hill. This seemingly misplaced geologic formation has over time served many purposes—as a fort, a public amusement center, and now as a quiet urban park. But what Baltimoreans appreciate most about Federal Hill is the spectacular view of downtown Baltimore and the Inner Harbor it reveals. The hill provides one of the greatest cityscapes in the country. The Waterfront Hike begins at Federal Hill Park, which perches atop Federal Hill.

1
Begin the hike atop Federal Hill.

The term Federal Hill is used to indicate both the hill and the adjoining neighborhood. The name Federal Hill derived from a party. In 1788, to celebrate Maryland's ratification of the federal Constitution, a raucous revelry was held on this hill. Large amounts of beer, cider ale, and meats were consumed, and cries of "Chutzpah for the Constitution" echoed across the city. Ever since that day, the red clay mound abutting Baltimore's harbor was known as Federal Hill.

Federal Hill later served military duty during the Civil War, when a fort kept watchful eye over the downtown district. Guns were pointed on the city to deter aggression from Southern sympathizers. Following its military discharge, the hill became a well-used urban park offering a wonderful view of the city. Today, Federal Hill anchors one of Baltimore's most desirable gentrified neighborhoods, and its primary use is as a playground for children and dogs.

Tunnels Beneath the Hill

A vast labyrinth of tunnels, centered deep beneath Federal Hill, fan out beneath the adjoining neighborhoods like tentacles of an octopus. The tunnels are hand-dug, but their specific origins remain unclear. Conventional wisdom says they are relics of a mining operation dating back to the early 1700s. High-quality sand and clay, ideal for terra-cotta and glassware, were probably excavated there. The bulk of the material probably went to construct local rowhouses. During the Civil War, the caverns were used to store artillery and other military gear. A cache of Civil War-era grenades was discovered beneath the hill in the 1920s. Following the war, civilians took advantage of the tunnels' perennially cool fifty-degree temperatures to store meats, sauerkrauts, and supposedly kegs and kegs of ale. Vagrants were known to disappear into the tunnels for days at a time, only to emerge in a drunken stupor. The most remarkable tunnel tale happened in 1920, when a band of neighborhood boys, searching one of the caverns for a lost ball, happened upon an Egyptian mummy entombed in a wooden casket. Instead of revealing their find, they collected the individual bones as souvenirs, giving some to their friends. An important archeological discovery, being stored for sale to a museum, was reduced to an empty casket. Today, the tunnels remain sealed to prevent entry.

2

Walk to the north face of Federal Hill, which faces downtown Baltimore.

Federal Hill offers sweeping views of Baltimore in three directions, and regularly garners the "Best View of Baltimore" award in local publications. To the north, facing the waterfront, is the glitzy bustle known as the Inner Harbor. Baltimore has the geographic advantage of having a downtown that hugs tight its waterfront, creating a festive and dynamic tourist attraction. Along the waterfront is an interesting ensemble of office buildings, shops, restaurants, a world-class aquarium—and on nice days a wonderful kaleidoscope of people.

Rash Field is situated at the north foot of Federal Hill, between Key Highway and the marina. It was once the football stadium of nearby Southern High School, but has since been reclaimed for use as public space. It's home to an ice rink in the winter. At the east end of Rash Field is a meticulously landscaped garden with a large wooden mast protruding from its center. This display is a memorial to the captain and three crew members who perished in the capsizing of the *Pride of Baltimore*. The *Pride* was Baltimore's good-will ship, a clipper schooner that logged over 150,000 miles circumnavigating the globe, promoting Baltimore to over 125 cities. In 1986, while traveling about 250 miles north of Puerto Rico, it was struck by a violent squall and capsized, claiming the four lives. Eight other crew members were rescued by a passing Norwegian tanker.

Urban Revitalization

Baltimore's Inner Harbor remains the poster child for successful urban redevelopment. As late as the 1960s, the derelict waterfront was considered a disgrace—a cesspool of raw sewage, rats, flotsam, and deserted wharves. The metamorphosis began in 1969, when the naval sloop *Constellation* was given its permanent home here. Then came a rash of office building construction, culminating with the World Trade Center in 1977. A convention center was built one block to the west. But it wasn't until July 2, 1980, that the Inner Harbor became a destination spot for residents and tourists alike, and the waterfront area could be officially labeled "reborn." That was the day that Harborplace was christened, complete with thirty-seven eating places, twenty food markets, forty-five specialty shops, and about thirty kiosks. Developed by James Rouse, and under the sponsorship of then-Mayor William Donald Schaefer, Harborplace caught the eye of the world—as a way to potentially reverse the urban exodus and attract tourists to the cities. Many waterfront cities nationwide have copied Baltimore's idea.

3
Walk to the east face of Federal Hill,
which faces the channel leading to the Chesapeake Bay.

Sprawled to the east of Federal Hill is the port of Baltimore. This is Baltimore's salty backbone, all but invisible to Inner Harbor visitors. The high-arched bridge in the distance is the Francis Scott Key Memorial Bridge, which carries the Baltimore beltway across the Patapsco River. It was from a boat near the site of this bridge that Francis Scott Key penned the lyrics to "The Star Spangled Banner." Also visible in the distance are the cranes of Baltimore's myriad port facilities, and the massive Bethlehem Steel plant exhaling billows of smoke.

The Domino Sugar plant is located on the south bank of the channel exiting the Inner Harbor. Its three-story neon red sign casts a comforting glow over South Baltimore, reminding viewers that industry is still alive in the city. It's said that this is the largest neon sign in the world. The "D" stands at thirty-two feet tall, and the entire sign employs 3,200 feet of handmade neon tubes. On most days, freighters from the Caribbean deposit raw sugar at Domino Sugar's dock. Domino Sugar processes 6.3 million pounds of sugar here each day.

Along the north shore, and just across the channel from Federal Hill, is a leveled property bordered by a marina. This is the former site of the Allied Signal plant, a chromium plant that gained notoriety for being on the Environmental Protection Agency's list of most critical Superfund sites. A recent $100 million dollar remediation project covered the contaminated soil, rendering it harmless. The real estate now lies fallow, awaiting redevelopment.

Visible behind the Allied Signal property is the mosaic of ethnic communities that are responsible for Baltimore's moniker "The City of Neighborhoods." Several of these neighborhoods are on this hike route. The enclave of institutional buildings high on the distant hill is Johns

Hopkins Hospital, perennially considered one of the best in the world by *U.S. News and World Report*. For perspective, find the gold onion-shaped domes located just below the Johns Hopkins Hospital complex; this is St. Michael's Ukranian Catholic Church, located in the neighborhood of Canton, which is the turnaround point for this hike.

At the base of the northeast corner of Federal Hill is the American Visionary Art Museum. This unique institution promotes the intuitive works of self-taught artists, often featuring works that deviate from what some may consider mainstream art. Immediately to the right of the museum is a forty-foot-tall wind-powered contraption called "Wind Sculpture," which was developed by a seventy-six-year-old mechanic and farmer named Vollis Simpson. His purpose in contriving this spectacle was to salute Federal Hill, and the concepts of life, liberty, and the pursuit of happiness.

4

Walk to the west face of Federal Hill, which fronts its namesake neighborhood.

This sweeping view over Federal Hill's rooftops and church steeples is a beautiful urban landscape. Standing atop the flight of stairs leading to the street below, notice the terrific telescopic view of Montgomery Street, which is among the most coveted addresses in the city. Here, reno-vated nineteenth-century rowhouses fetch upwards of $500,000. Prominent in the distance is Camden Yards—the collective term for the two stadiums serving Baltimore's professional sports teams. The more prominent facility to the left is Raven Stadium, easily recognizable by its purple seats. This is home to the Baltimore Ravens football team, which won the 2001 Super Bowl championship. To the right, and partially hidden by a concrete apartment building (look for the black light stands), is Oriole Park at Camden Yards, home of the Baltimore Orioles.

5

Descend the 100 steps on the west face of Federal Hill. At the bottom, turn right onto Battery Avenue and proceed for one block to Key Highway. Cross Key Highway and continue for about 200 feet to the brick waterfront promenade. Turn left onto the promenade.

Shortly after crossing Key Highway, notice, to the left, the Herschell Stillman Carousel. This 1912 amusement ride was restored to working condition in 1994 by a local high school, and draws the attention of children on summer days. Alongside the carousel is a screened-in weather station used by local television and radio stations to gauge atmospheric conditions around the harbor.

Just after turning left onto the promenade, note a sculpture of Japanese design. It's entitled "Yuai," and was a 1984 gift from Baltimore's sister city, Kawasaki, Japan, to commemorate the fifth anniversary of its sibling arrangement.

6

Follow the promenade to the right as it wraps around the waterfront in front of the Maryland Science Center.

The Maryland Science Center, and its super-screened Imax theater, is at the bend of the harbor's promenade. Directly across the promenade are the access docks for Baltimore's fleet of water taxis that transport guests—at a very reasonable price—to dozens of locations around the harbor. Riding a water taxi may be the best bargain in town. Around the corner from the Maryland Science Center, and to the left, is a diminutive statue of a penguin. The original home of this misplaced creature was the headquarters building of Penguin Books, a publisher once located in Baltimore. When the company left town, the penguin was given a new home along the waterfront. It was carved of Vermont marble in 1956 by Grace Turnbull.

The stretch of promenade along the terminus of the waterfront is the former steamship hub of Baltimore city. It was here where many of Baltimore's steamships were built, including the city's first, named the *Chesapeake*. In a previous era, crowds would gather here to board steamships that crossed the Chesapeake Bay to eastern shore ports. The trip would take two hours and twenty minutes, and set each passenger back seventeen cents.

Just past the Maryland Science Center and to the right are the docks of Baltimore's tall ship collection, which includes the *Clipper City*, sometimes the *Nighthawk*, and, if you are lucky, the *Pride of Baltimore II*. The *Pride II* was commissioned in 1988 to continue the mission of its sister ship, the first *Pride of Baltimore*, which was lost at sea. A bit farther is the mooring spot for the *Bay Lady* and *Lady Baltimore*, two charter cruise ships that motor the harbor's waters, hosting cruise parties.

The green-roofed building to the left is the Light Street Pavilion, which is part of the Harborplace development. It contains an array of eateries, specialty shops, and kiosks. This pavilion provides a refreshing hiking break. The landmark seafood restaurant known as Phillips Harborplace, rated as one of the busiest in the country, is located at the south end of the pavilion. Though the line for the main restaurant may be prohibitive, Phillips offers a kiosk-type stand in the pavilion.

7

Next to the *Constellation*, follow the promenade to the right as it wraps around the waterfront.

The 186-foot *Constellation* is a naval sloop of war that was launched in 1854. It's the only surviving Civil War-era naval vessel, and the last all-sail ship built by the U.S. Navy. Among the *Constellation*'s storied feats: it captured three slave-carrying ships en route to the United States, freeing over 1,000 Africans; it fought in the Mediterranean Sea, and later in the shipping lanes off Cuba, during the Civil War; and it transported famine relief to Ireland. The *Constellation* recently underwent a thirty-one-month, $7.5 million restoration, where, among other things, its rotting hull was replaced by a laminated shell. This was the largest non-naval wooden-ship restoration project ever in the United States.

Harborplace's Pratt Street Pavilion, immediately across the promenade from the *Constellation*, caught the theme and chain restaurant wave that swept over the harbor. It's home to such eateries as Planet Hollywood and the Cheesecake Factory. Many shops line its interior corridors.

Just past the pavilion is the World Trade Center, which is the tallest pentagonal-shaped building in the world. The

---

The Case of Mistaken Identity

The *Constellation* for a long while suffered from an identity crisis. It was long thought that this ship was the thirty-eight-gun U.S. Frigate *Constellation*, which was built in 1797 and fought valiantly during the War of 1812. After a circumnavigation of the globe, the frigate returned to port tired and decaying. She was relegated to the Gosport (now Norfolk) Naval Yard in Virginia for reconditioning. Soon after, a large warship—this one a sloop-of-war bearing the name *Constellation*—emerged from the same shipyard to embark on a stellar military career of its own. After battles with slave ships and warships, she was eventually moored in Baltimore's Inner Harbor. The question: Is this the same *Constellation* warship that was built in 1797, making it the oldest intact American naval ship? Or is it a newly fabricated ship built in 1854 at the Gosport Naval Yard that by happenstance carries the same name? Baltimore's "*Constellation* Committee" argued that it was indeed the original ship, modified only by a major overhaul. Other historians countered, saying no way possible. This debate went on for decades, and was not cleared up until 1991, when a report was published by the U.S. Navy's Curator of Ship Models, entitled "Fouled Anchors." The report revealed indisputable evidence of a hoax and coverup by those hoping for the 1797 construction date, including forged and altered documents. Artifacts from the ship were found to be tampered with. The conclusion: the *Constellation* resting idly in the Inner Harbor is a Civil War-era sloop built in 1854, and not a rebuilt 1797 frigate. Evidence later showed that while the original *Constellation* was being dismantled in the Gosport shipyard, about 600 feet away the new *Constellation* was being built. Mystery solved.

geometry of the World Trade Center is such that two sides come together at a point on the water, supposedly giving it the appearance of a ship's bow as seen from across the harbor. The twenty-eight-story tower has an observation deck on the twenty-seventh floor called the Top of the World, which provides not only spectacular views of Baltimore, but also information about Balitmore City and its port facilities. The building was designed by world-renowned architect I.M. Pei.

A plaque along the base of the World Trade Center remembers the ship *Exodus*. In 1947, a Baltimore-based Chesapeake Bay steamer ship snuck into southern France to secretly pick up 4,000 Jewish refugees with the intention of smuggling them into Palestine. En route, a British warship confronted the *Exodus*. A skirmish resulted, and the *Exodus* crew ultimately surrendered. The refugees were forcibly returned to their European camps. Public backlash from this incident led to the partition of Palestine and the establishment of the state of Israel. Leon Uris, a Baltimore native, penned the novel *Exodus* in commemoration of this event.

Docked just past the World Trade Center is the 133-foot *Lightship Chesapeake*, which was built in Charleston, South Carolina, in 1930. A lightship is essentially a floating lighthouse, and is usually anchored where placing a stationary lighthouse is not feasible. The *Lightship Chesapeake* initially sat off Fenwick Island in Delaware. In 1933, it was moved to the mouth of the Chesapeake Bay, where it served admirably until 1965, when it was replaced by a platform light. It was then transferred to the mouth of the Delaware Bay until 1970 when, once again, a permanent structure rendered it obsolete. The *Lightship Chesapeake* has since been a tourist attraction.

Anchored behind the *Lightship Chesapeake* is the USS *Torsk*, which is one of two surviving Tench-class fleet submarines in the nation (the other is docked in Pittsburgh, Pennsylvania). The *Torsk* was built in Portsmouth, New Hampshire, and launched in September 1944. It patrolled the waters of the Pacific Ocean during World War II, entering that theater via the Panama Canal. The *Torsk* has the distinction of firing the last torpedo, and sinking the final Japanese vessel, of World War II. A November 28, 2000, feature story on Inner Harbor attractions in *The Sun* states that the *Torsk* has made 11,884 dives, more than any other submarine.

The polychromatic concrete and steel angular building, just past the World Trade Center, is perhaps Baltimore's best-known—and most photographed—attraction. The National Aquarium in Baltimore opened its doors in August 1981, and has since hosted more than twenty-two million visitors. The aquarium houses upwards of 10,000 marine and freshwater critters in over one million gallons of water. The top floor, visible through the slanted glass, is a walk-through tropical rainforest display. For an interesting hike diversion, walk a few paces past the aquarium's main entrance to the always entertaining, and free of charge, seal tank.

Just past the aquarium and straight ahead is the Power Plant, easily identifiable by its four prominent smokestacks. In a previous era, this was a generation plant that powered the streetcars that roamed Baltimore's downtown. Over the past ten years, it has endured two failed attempts at development—one as a Six Flags indoor amusement center and the other as a dance club. Today, it has settled into a comfortable niche as a venue for some of the harbor's most popular shops and restaurants, including the ESPN Zone, Barnes & Noble, and the Hard Rock Café. It's worth a moment's time to step inside the bookstore to view the restored copper-painted furnaces and the walls decorated with historical photographs of Baltimore. Guitar buffs may notice that the sixty-eight-foot neon guitar slung atop the Power Plant is a McCarty model, and not a Fender or Gibson that caps all other Hard Rock Cafés.

8
Cross the footbridge immediately in front of the Power Plant building. Veer right, cutting between the aquarium's Marine Mammal Pavilion and Surfside Sally's.

The Marine Mammal Pavilion opened in 1990 and is home to an amphitheater where dolphin shows are conducted. It's connected to the main aquarium by an over-water walkway. A plaque at the base of the Marine Mammal Pavilion announces the burial of a time capsule to be opened in 2090.

9

**Cross a second footbridge just past the Marine Mammal
Pavilion. Continue straight ahead on the road that runs
between the Columbus Center to the left
and the Pier 5 Hotel to the right.**

To the left, and resting peacefully from an exhausting
career, is the U.S. Coast Guard Cutter *Taney*. The *Taney* was
commissioned in 1936 and served in the Pacific theater
during World War II. It is the only ship still afloat that
survived the Pearl Harbor bombardment. The *Taney* later
engaged in the Okinawa campaign. In its post-military existence, the *Taney* served as a weather ship, a military training
vessel, and a member of the Amelia Earhart search party. Its
final voyage involved tracking down waterborne drug
traders. The *Taney* was decommissioned in 1986.

Just past the footbridge is the exclusive Pier 5 Hotel. On
display immediately behind the hotel is an actual Chesapeake
Bay lighthouse that was brought here during the harbor's
revitalization. Across from the hotel, beneath the waves of
white canopy, is the Columbus Center. This institute was
built in 1995 for the purpose of dovetailing the concepts of
research, education, and tourism—specifically in the area of
marine biotechnology. Though it never caught on as a tourist
attraction, it still harbors several research firms. Just past the
Columbus Center is the Pier 6 Concert Pavilion, where on
summer evenings music from big-name acts suffuse with
the harbor's melodies.

10

**Cross over a third footbridge, which leads to President
Street. Turn right onto President Street.
Continue on President Street for one block.**

Just across the footbridge, the spectacular and eclecti-
cally designed building to the right is, of all things, a sewage
pumping station. This may very well be the most attractive
sewage pumping station in the nation. Henry Brauns
designed the Edwardian structure, which was built in 1912.
Its roof reflects an ornate Victorian design. The Baltimore

Public Works Museum inhabits the southwest quadrant of the building, with an outdoor interpretive exhibit called "streetscape sculpture" showing the cross-section of a typical Baltimore street. Notice the statue of Christopher Columbus to the left, next to the pumping station.

11
Turn left onto Fleet Street.
Continue on Fleet Street for two blocks.

On the corner of President and Fleet streets stands the President Street Station, which is thought to be the oldest surviving urban railroad terminal in the United States. It was also one of the first public buildings in the country to have an arched roof. The President Street Station now serves as the Civil War Museum. This train station played a prominent role in the first blood shed in the Civil War. Soon after the attack on Fort Sumter, Union soldiers arrived at the President Street Station en route to Washington, D.C. As they disembarked and walked to Camden Station, located about a mile to the west, they were ambushed by a local cadre of southern sympathizers. Several were killed in the first of many historical instances that dubbed Baltimore "Mobtown."

12
Turn right onto Exeter Street, heading toward the water-
front promenade. Turn left onto the waterfront promenade.
Continue on the promenade for about two blocks.

This promenade heads toward Fells Point. This area between the Inner Harbor and Fells Point is swelling from intense developmental pressure, with new bars, businesses, and one of the largest hotels in Baltimore under construction. Across the canal from the Sylvan Learning Center is the Living Classrooms Foundation, an educational organization focusing on at-risk youth. The foundation runs about thirty-five programs ranging from schooner building to mathematics, and caters to over 50,000 students annually. Many of the classes are conducted on ships. It is not unusual to see the students tooling around the waters of the canal in either rowboats or sailboats.

13
**The promenade becomes Lancaster Street.
Continue straight on Lancaster Street across Caroline
Street and into the Fells Point neighborhood.**

Across Caroline Street is the historic district of Fells Point, which is Baltimore's nautical hub. Fells Point may contain the city's largest concentration of pubs and bars, making it Baltimore's premier weekend party spot. The back streets of Fells Point are lined with some of the city's oldest rowhouses that reflect a 200-year-old quaintness and charm. Most are well kept, adorned with flower boxes, marble steps, and interesting architectural features. And if the wind is blowing just right, the sweet cinnamon fragrance of the H&S Bakery, a large commercial operation located a few blocks to the north, mingles with the sea air.

Nautical Charm

If Baltimore is indeed a "sailor's town," then Fells Point is the bar. This charming waterfront community has for centuries remained steadfast to its maritime (and drinking) roots. Fells Point was named for the English land speculator William Fell, who in 1726 purchased the peninsula on which the present neighborhood rests. With its natural deep water port, Fells Point became the focal point of Baltimore's trade, and served as the original port of Baltimore for over 100 years. In the 1800s, shipbuilding came to the peninsula, and over eighteen shipyards lined the waterfront, turning out hundreds of vessels of varying types. The most symbolic of Baltimore was the topsail schooner known as the Baltimore Clipper. It was a popular commercial and warship, showing greater speed and maneuverability than most warships of that era. When port operations shifted elsewhere following the Civil War, Fells Point evolved into a clutch of bars and brothels and boarding houses, frequented mostly by sailors. Today, Fells Point remains mostly a haven of bars and cafés and interesting boutiques, though its present clientele tend to be more upscale. Its nautical essence, however, remains undaunted.

14

Continue on Lancaster Street for four blocks past Caroline Street. Turn right onto Broadway. Continue on Broadway for one block, until it dead-ends at the waterfront.

Broadway is the main thoroughfare of Fells Point. Unique shops and pubs line its cobbled street. Perhaps the most popular is Bertha's, located on the corner of Lancaster Street and Broadway. Bertha's serves seafood to some of Baltimore's most demanding palates. Its ubiquitous bumper stickers that encourage people to "Eat Bertha's Mussels" have been a mainstay on Baltimore cars for years.

The Admiral Fell Inn stands at 888 South Broadway. It was established in 1892 by a Christian organization known as the Women's Auxiliary of the Port Mission. Its purpose was to offer lodging to visiting sailors without the lure of liquor or women. Cots were available for thirty-five cents. At that time, the mission was called the Anchorage, and nicknamed the Doghouse. It later became a YMCA, and then a vinegar factory. Today it's an elegant inn.

Broadway Pier stands at the foot of Broadway. This was an important entry point for immigrants passing through Locust Point, which is just across the water. The Locust Point Ferry regularly deposited the new arrivals here. When Meg Ryan made her first appearance in *Sleepless in Seattle*, she was walking on this pier. The hulking brick complex across the harbor is the Domino Sugar plant. The smaller brick building to the left is the former Procter & Gamble plant, where Joy, Ivory, Dawn, and Tide were produced. It's now a business park called Tide Point Waterfront Park.

15

**Turn left onto Thames Street.
Continue on Thames Street for one block.**

More bars, more pubs, more cafés, more boutiques. Names like Cat's Eye Pub, John Stevens Ltd., the Admiral Fell Inn, and the Waterfront quickly become indelible to memory. A saloon called The Horse You Came in On is located in the 1600 block of Thames Street. English mystery writer Martha Grimes visited this pub and became so fascinated with its name she titled her next novel after it.

The large brick edifice to the right is known as Recreation Pier. If a sense of déjà vu strikes, it's because this building has appeared hundreds of times on television. Recreation Pier for years served as the makeshift police headquarters for the critically acclaimed televison drama *Homicide: Life on the Street*. The show was based on a book by Baltimore writer David Simon, that detailed life as a Baltimore cop. It was entirely set and filmed in Baltimore, and wholeheartedly embraced by the community. It was not unusual to see such *Homicide* actors as Ned Beatty, Andre Braugher, Daniel Baldwin, and Richard Belzer frequenting local pubs.

16
Turn right onto Fell Street.
Continue on Fell Street for one block.

Most of the waterfront warehouses along Fell Street are tony condominiums, but each comes with a significant past. Belt's Wharf, across from where Wolfe Street enters, was where imported coffee was housed. Henderson's Wharf, located just beyond Belt's Wharf, was where tobacco was stored awaiting export to Europe. Swann's Wharf, located across Fell Street from Henderson's Wharf, was the office of Thomas Swann, former mayor of Baltimore and governor of Maryland. It also served as a temporary prison for Confederate soldiers during the Civil War. Swann's Wharf was built in 1845, and the other two warehouses date to the late nineteenth century.

17
Turn left onto Wolfe Street.
Continue on Wolfe Street for three blocks.

Just past Lancaster Street and to the right is a warehouse belonging to the National Aquarium in Baltimore. This is where they keep equipment for their Marine Animal Rescue Program. The rescue truck is sometimes parked here.

18

**Turn right onto Aliceanna Street.
Continue on Aliceanna Street for about one-quarter mile.**

19

At the Captain James Restaurant, which is shaped like the fore hull of a ship, turn right onto Boston Street. Continue on Boston Street for four blocks.

The neighborhood of Canton begins just past Captain James Restaurant. Canton is where Baltimore's latest broad-scale revitalization project is happening. What used to be derelict warehouses and industrial buildings are becoming chic condos and businesses. Boston Street was once called "Cannery Row" for the many canneries that lined its waterfront. Now, it's referred to as the "Golden Mile" for the concentration of wealth that has settled here. The neighborhood of Canton can be explored in depth in the East Baltimore Hike.

20

Turn left onto Montford Avenue. Continue on Montford Avenue for four blocks, until it dead-ends at Eastern Avenue.

Before turning left, notice the high-rise residential building on Boston Street along the waterfront. This is Anchorage Towers, and beside it are forty-eight townhouse units, each facing the harbor. Built in 1982, this project started Canton's rise to prosperity. It was conceived of by then-Mayor William Donald Schaefer, whose attention was grabbed by a similar waterfront arrangement while visiting Boston.

Montford Avenue reveals many signature elements of Baltimore that have remained static over time. The gray building material on the rowhouses is formstone, which is actually a fabricated covering created to protect the brick and make the house watertight. It was the rage in the 1950s and '60s. Look for marble stoops and stained glass windows, such as those on house numbers 707 through 711. Corner pubs, crab houses, and package good stores are plentiful through this section of Canton.

On the corner of Montford and Eastern avenues is the stuccoed majesty of St. Michael the Archangel Ukrainian Catholic Church. The congregation opened this sanctuary in 1991 after moving from Wolfe Street in Fells Point. The building was constructed in the shape of a Greek cross. Services are given in both English and Ukrainian.

21

Turn left onto Eastern Avenue. Continue on Eastern Avenue into downtown Baltimore. [Option: add a one-half-mile loop to the hike through Patterson Park by crossing over Eastern Avenue and proceeding up the stairs into the park. Walk straight ahead on the path about one-quarter mile to the Pagoda, then backtrack down the hill to this point.]

The 155-acre Patterson Park is supposedly Baltimore's busiest park. It is the former estate of William Patterson, and was opened to the public in 1853. The park carries a rich history. In the early nineteenth century, waterfront residents retreated here to escape the yellow fever. During the War of 1812, fortifications here fended off British attack. During the Civil War, the park harbored a temporary hospital for soldiers wounded at Gettysburg. Today it is a recreational park offering an assortment of playing fields, an Olympic-sized swimming pool, a hockey rink, a community center, and a 2.6-acre pond.

The Patterson Park Observatory is also known as the Pagoda. It was designed by Charles Latrobe and built in 1891. The sixty-foot-tall octagonal structure was just renovated and offers panoramic views of East Baltimore and the Chesapeake Bay. The five cannons beside the Pagoda were used to successfully fend off the British during the Battle of North Point in 1814.

Eastern Avenue straddles the neighborhoods of Butchers Hill to the right and Fells Point to the left. Notice how the saloons and shops along Eastern Avenue become more upscale approaching Broadway. Corner pubs like Boots Saloon yield to more trendy antique centers and coffee shops. The reason some store signage is in Spanish is because this neighborhood is the home to Baltimore's burgeoning Hispanic community.

The Patterson Bowling Center stands at 2105 Eastern Avenue. This is one of the few remaining duckpin bowling alleys in Baltimore. The game was invented in 1900 by Wilbert Robinson and John McGraw, members of the original Baltimore Orioles, who owned Diamond Alleys on Howard Street. Duckpin bowlers roll a five-inch ball at short, squat pins. The sport is unique to Maryland and seven other states. The Patterson Bowling Center has stood here since 1927 and features twelve lanes (six on each floor).

22
Continue on Eastern Avenue, past Broadway.

Cross Broadway, and look left to see the Broadway Market, which is one of Baltimore's seven city-operated markets. Broadway Market dates to 1784, predating incorporation of the city itself.

Across Broadway is what may be called Little Poland, due to the large number of Polish immigrants who once settled here. Though the ethnic makeup of the neighborhood has changed, vestiges of the Polish heritage remain. The Polish Home Club, which was built in 1906 as a social club, stands at 510-12 Broadway. The former Polish National Alliance Club Council 21, another Polish social club, stands at 1627 Eastern Avenue. Kosciuszko Federal Savings Bank, at 1635 Eastern Avenue, was established in 1894 by, among others, Barbara Mikulski's grandfather, Michael Kutz, to loan money to Polish immigrants. (Barbara Mikulski went on to forge a career in politics that took her to the U.S. Senate.) It was named for Thaddeus Kosciuszko, a Polish Revolutionary War hero. Across the street is Anna's Delicatessen, which serves authentic Polish cuisine.

23
Continue on Eastern Avenue past Central Avenue.

24
Continue on Eastern Avenue for one block past Central Avenue. Turn right onto Exeter Street. Continue on Exeter Street for three blocks. It will veer left after one block.

Across Central Avenue begins the popular neighborhood of Little Italy, where hungry Baltimoreans come on weekends for their pasta fix. Unlike Little Poland, this neighborhood has passed through the ages relatively unfettered, remaining Italian through and through. Homes are still passed down through the generations (there are few, if any, "For Sale" signs here), and the sweet aroma of marinara sauce still fills the alley streets. Exeter Street is a fair representation of the enclave's ethnicity. Red, green, and white flags and banners often flap in the breeze, and religious icons grace the windows. Gardens are hidden throughout the neighborhood, on the rooftops and in the patio yards.

Genoese immigrants first arrived in Little Italy starting in the early 1800s. Most passed through en route to the western part of the country. Those who stayed, however, turned this cluster of rowhouses into one of Baltimore's most unique and festive communities. No less than twenty traditional Italian restaurants line the streets, and Italian markets still provide fresh pasta and imported Italian food. Annual street festivals such as St. Anthony's Day in June and St. Gabriel's Day in August showcase the residents' steadfast allegiance to their heritage. On weekends, the streets are burdened with throngs of hungry restaurant patrons, and in summers an outdoor movie series adds to the festive atmosphere.

25
Turn left onto Stiles Street. Continue on Stiles Street for four blocks until it dead-ends at President Street.

St. Leo's Church sits at the northeast corner of Exeter and Stiles streets. Built in 1881, it was the first church in Baltimore constructed by and for Italian immigrants. When Little Italy stretched from the harbor to Broadway, this church had 2,400 members (the community has since been reduced to about twelve square blocks). St. Leo's still offers a weekly mass in Italian.

One block down Stiles Street are the courts of the Little Italy Bocce Rollers Association. Local residents gather here on pleasant evenings to socialize and compete. Italian is the preferred language of the courts. Perhaps a bocce court and balls may be available to use; or better yet, take a breather and watch the local pros roll.

Just past the bocce courts is High Street. This street hosts the primary concentration of well-known restaurants. In the space of a few blocks is Sabatino's, Ciao Bella, Chiaparelli's, Da Mimmo, and Ceaser's Den, whose names long ago became Baltimore traditions. Sabatino's may be the best place in Baltimore to spot a celebrity. One block ahead, on the corner of Stiles and Albemarle streets, is Vaccaro's pastry and dessert shop, at which many Little Italy diners either finish their meal or should have. This is the perfect pit-stop for pastry or gelato (Italian ice cream).

26
Turn right onto President Street. Continue on President Street for one block.

27
Turn left onto Pratt Street. Continue on Pratt Street for two blocks.

Before turning left, look north on President Street. Two prominent steeple-like structures compete for attention. One is a 234-foot-high circular red brick tower. This is the Shot

Tower, which was built in 1828—interestingly, without the use of scaffolding. It is where lead shot was manufactured. Molten lead was poured in drops from the top of the tower, forming a ball during its descent. The mass then solidified when it hit a pool of cool water at the tower's base. This tower produced one-half million bags of lead shot each year. It is one of the few remaining shot towers in existence.

The white steeple to the left of the Shot Tower belongs to St. Vincent de Paul Church. The three-tiered steeple is 150 feet tall, and is capped with a dome and cross. It's constructed of brick, but was created and painted to resemble wood. The church was built around 1841.

The dark red building along President Street, just before the Shot Tower, was the main exhibition hall of the Baltimore City Life Museums. All buildings that comprised the museum, including this one, were put up for sale in 1997 when the city was unable to pay its debt on them. The attractive cast-iron facade of this particular building once adorned the G. Fava Fruit Company building, which stood along Pratt Street near the location of Baltimore's Convention Center.

28
Just past the Power Plant, and in front of the National Aquarium, move left onto the brick waterfront promenade.

29
Continue on the waterfront promenade, wrapping around the Inner Harbor.

30
This hike ends back at the foot of Federal Hill.

Suggested Reading

Books

Wish You Were Here! A Guide to Baltimore City for Natives and Newcomers by Carolyn Males, Carol Barbier Rolnick, and Pam Makowski Goresh

A Guide to Baltimore Architecture by John Dorsey and James D. Dilts

Walking in Baltimore: An Intimate Guide to the Old City by Frank R. Shivers, Jr.

Baltimore: The Building of an American City by Sherry H. Olson

The Baltimore Rowhouse by Mary Ellen Hayward and Charles Belfoure

Websites

Baltimore City Government
www.ci.baltimore.md.us

Port of Baltimore
www.mpa.state.md.us

Live Baltimore Home Center
www.livebaltimore.com

Welcome to Harborplace
www.harborplace.com

Peninsula

Latrobe Park Terrace, Locust Point

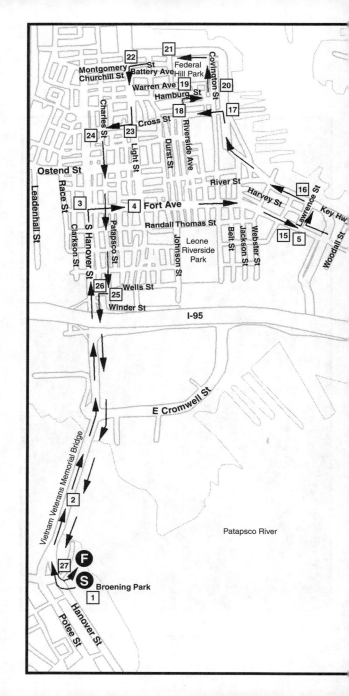

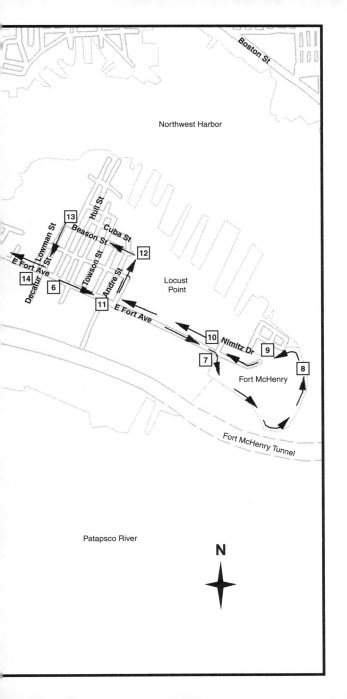

Overview

Distance: Eight-and-one-half miles. Note that this hike can be shortened by almost three miles by parking near the corner of Fort Avenue and Hanover Street in South Baltimore, and starting with direction number three. See map for details.

Major attractions: The neighborhoods of South Baltimore, Locust Point, and Federal Hill; and the Fort McHenry National Monument.

Starting location: The public parking lot at Broening Park, adjacent to the northwest side of Harbor Hospital, in South Baltimore. The lot offers free parking, and is used primarily by boaters and fishermen on the Middle Branch of the Patapsco River.

Directions to start and parking: From Baltimore city, take Hanover Street south. Cross the Vietnam Veterans Memorial Bridge (formerly, the Hanover Street Bridge) over the Middle Branch of the Patapsco River. At the first light past the bridge, turn left onto Waterview Avenue. Continue on Waterview Avenue for one block. At the light, continue straight into the public parking lot at Broening Park.

From the south, approach Baltimore on I-95. Take Exit 54, Hanover Street, which is the first exit past I-395. Continue south on Hanover Street, across the Vietnam Veterans Memorial Bridge. From there, follow the directions above.

Access to eating facilities: Restaurants and convenience stores are scattered across the three neighborhoods covered in the Peninsula Hike. The greatest concentrations are along Fort Avenue through South Baltimore and Locust Point; and along Light Street and Charles Street in Federal Hill.

Introduction

South Baltimore's peninsula, which juts into the Patapsco River, contains the neighborhoods of Locust Point, South Baltimore, and Federal Hill—all of which are explored on this hike. One of the purposes of this book is to introduce hikers to some of Baltimore's lesser-known communities— ones that aren't often frequented, but that have a special attribute or fascination, such as Locust Point. It could be called a hidden jewel. Not for having fine dining or fancy rowhouses or trendy boutiques. Not for being touristy or gentrified. Locust Point is a jewel because it probably reveals better than any community what it was like to live in Baltimore City a century ago. Things have changed very little in Locust Point (although gentrification is starting to take hold). The residential community is still quiet, friendly, and proud. The rail yards still envelop the peninsula, and massive container ships still drop anchor in the port facilities. The community of Locust Point has worked hard to retain its character and charm. The area also contains what may be the most interesting mile in the city—the paved walking loop around the perimeter of the Fort McHenry National Monument, which offers a unique perspective of Baltimore's waterfront. At over eight miles, this is the book's longest hike, but any Baltimorean would agree that it's also one of the most fascinating.

1

Begin the hike in the public parking lot adjacent to the northwest side of Harbor Hospital. Follow the parking lot driveway to the road. Turn right onto Hanover Street, heading toward downtown Baltimore. Continue on Hanover Street across the Vietnam Veterans Memorial Bridge.

Near the entrance to the parking lot is Maryland's Vietnam Veterans Memorial. It was dedicated in 1989 to commemorate those Marylanders who served in, are missing from, or lost their lives in the Vietnam War. The names of the thirty-five Marylanders who remain missing, and the 1,046 who lost their lives, are inscribed on a granite bench around the monument's circumference. Each of the sixteen spires represents one year that the war was fought. This location was selected for the monument because of its peaceful perch overlooking the Patapsco River. The existence of the memorial can be attributed to "The Last Patrol"—a group of Vietnam War veterans who did several long-distance walks around Maryland to garner support for the memorial. Their longest walk was 365 miles, from the town of Oakland, in western Maryland's mountains, to Ocean City on the shore.

2

Cross over the Vietnam Veterans Memorial Bridge.

The Vietnam Veterans Memorial Bridge spans, and offers wonderful views of, the Middle Branch of the Patapsco River. Hanover Street—and Ritchie Highway, as it's called south of the city—was contemplated as a grand boulevard connecting Baltimore with cities to the south. The bridge was built in 1914 as the showpiece of the boulevard, providing a dramatic entrance to downtown Baltimore. The problem was that obtaining the right-of-way to build the road required guarantees to the local property owners of development along its route. Instead of becoming an attractive showpiece boulevard, Hanover Street and Ritchie Highway have turned into a stretch of commercial enterprises. Hanover Street has the distinction of being the first dual-lane, high-speed road in Baltimore.

Look out over the Middle Branch of the Patapsco River. According to Robert C. Keith in *Baltimore Harbor: A Picture History*, had Baltimore's forefathers had their way, this setting would be one of skyscrapers and tourist attractions instead of industrial parks. This is where the founding fathers of Baltimore originally intended to develop downtown Baltimore. They found it more desirable than the swampy tract around what is now the Inner Harbor. Their plan was thwarted when John Moale, a landowner along the Middle Branch, successfully argued to the state legislature that mining was more important to the establishment of a city than land speculation, and that mining activities did not exist around the Middle Branch (but did, around what is now Locust Point and elsewhere). As a result, Middle Branch today is rimmed with industries and parks, and not parking garages and businesses.

Cross the bridge and note the area to the left, once known as Spring Garden Channel, named for the many springs that once freshened the river. Gwynns Falls flows into the Middle Branch beneath the tangle of highway to the far side. The red-roofed building on the south bank of the channel is the Baltimore Rowing and Water Resource Center, home to the Baltimore Rowing Club. Rowing shells and sculls can be seen slicing through the sheltered waters of the Middle Branch in the early mornings and late afternoons. The club attracts a wide range of oarsmen, from novices to elite. The rowing center is also used for city and private functions. The manufacturing plant at the far end of the waterway is a glassworks factory.

The area to the right of the bridge, on the far shore, is known as Port Covington. The peninsula jutting into the Middle Branch from Port Covington is known as Ferry Bar Point. It was here that numerous swimming resorts sprang up in the late nineteenth century—before pollution took its toll on the river. The most popular was called George Kahl's Ferry Bar, which featured a restaurant, bathing facilities, and an electric launch that took patrons to other resorts along the shore. Masses of pleasure-seekers leisurely drifted in rafts and rowboats and inner tubes here. The stretch of shoreline on the south side of the Middle Branch, now occupied by Harbor Hospital, was a popular public bathing beach. Ferry Bar Point was also the location of Fort Babcock, which served during the War of 1812.

The Vietnam Veterans Memorial Bridge was not the first to cross the Middle Branch. In 1856, a wooden bridge spanned the waterway from the tip of Ferry Bar Point to what is now the hospital grounds. The bridge was an extension of Light Street.

In addition to the swimming resorts, many yacht and rowing clubs dotted this shoreline. The sport of rowing experienced an increase in popularity in the early 1900s. That was during an era when rowing races were fodder for gamblers. Two now defunct rowing clubs—the Aerial Rowing Club and Arundel Boat Club—operated from boathouses along this shoreline. The present-day Baltimore Rowing Club memorializes this bygone era of rowing by hosting the Aerial Regatta each fall, in which rowers from up and down the East Coast compete.

As you come off the bridge, note the two substantial industries to the right. The brick building is home to Locke Insulators, which is among the nation's leading producers of porcelain insulators. The white building farther along Hanover Street is where *The Sun,* Baltimore's daily newspaper, is printed. A shopping center is also located here.

Beyond the Vietnam Veterans Memorial Bridge to the left is McComas Street, which terminates at a small plot of grass along the waterfront, known as Swann Park. This is where nearby Southern High School plays many of its sporting events. This park was home to a former local baseball team called "Johnny's" that groomed such big-league sluggers as Al Kaline and Reggie Jackson. The block of seven rowhouses at the foot of McComas Street may comprise Baltimore's smallest neighborhood.

3

Continue on Hanover Street, across the exit ramps to I-95. In just over one-half mile, turn right onto Fort Avenue. Continue on Fort Avenue through South Baltimore and Locust Point.

Fort Avenue is a main thoroughfare of South Baltimore. It was once the neighborhood's premier shopping district, though now it's mostly lined with tiny rowhouses, corner pubs, and convenience stores. The long brick building to the right between Marshall and Light streets is a former bowling alley that was later a post office. It now contains four condominium units. Looking left down Light Street, you will see the brick building at 1427 Light Street, which is the School 33 Art Center. It was built in 1880 as an elementary school, but was converted in 1979 to artists' studios and galleries. The galleries at times are open for viewing.

4

Continue on Fort Avenue past Light Street.

5

Continue on Fort Avenue past Lawrence Street. Stay on the right side of Fort Avenue through Locust Point.

The restaurant Rallos stands at the corner of Fort Avenue and Lawrence Street. This family-owned eatery has served the neighborhood for over sixty years. It is one of Baltimore's few restaurants that can be deemed "institutions." Its specialty is inexpensive, home-style food.

The neighborhood of Locust Point begins just past Rallos. Most people know Locust Point as home to the Fort McHenry National Monument, but its history runs much deeper. Besides being one of Baltimore's most important commercial ports, Locust Point was also the second largest destination point for immigrants entering the United States, behind only Ellis Island in New York City. German, Polish, Irish, and Ukrainian immigrants by the thousands settled here in the nineteenth and early twentieth centuries. Five and six generations later, their descendants remain, occupying the same tiny rowhouses. Locust Point is one of the classic neighborhoods in Baltimore City.

Southside Marketplace sits at the intersection of Lawrence Street and Fort Avenue. It was built in 1992 on the grounds of the former Buck Glass factory. The vacant warehouse just past the shopping center once belonged to the White Lead Company, which shows up on an 1869 map of the peninsula. It is one of the earliest known industries on Locust Point. Behind the warehouse are the staging grounds for the MARC commuter trains that serve Baltimore and Washington, D.C. A few blocks past the warehouse is Woodall Street, named for a shipbuilding company that operated from the foot of the street along the Inner Harbor.

The right side of Fort Avenue is lined with several industries, most of which have closed their doors. The former Chesapeake Paperboard Company, located at Woodall Street, made paper products, and later was a recycling plant. Just beyond Chesapeake Paperboard is the former Coca-Cola bottling plant, secure behind a silver security gate. It was built in 1926, and was once said to have housed one of the four known copies of the secret Coca-Cola formula.

Just past Armour Street and to the left, notice the basement windows on the block of houses from 1230 to 1244 East Fort Avenue. The windows appear to sink into the ground the closer the house is to the railroad bridge. This is because the elevation of Fort Avenue had to be raised slightly to accommodate construction of the railroad bridge. The railroad was put in place in the 1850s, replacing what was Jones Street. This allows access to the coal piers and grain elevators of the port of Baltimore. The railroad route through Locust Point is circuitous, with this stretch of track serving outgoing trains.

Just past the railroad bridge to the left, 1318 East Fort Avenue is a former movie theater. It opened in 1942 as the Flag Theater, and was later called the Deluxe Theatre. This theater has the distinction of being one of the first in the city to feature air conditioning. On the theater's side wall along Lowman Street, notice the peeling wall advertisement touting air conditioning. The theater closed in 1959.

Farther along Fort Avenue is the Francis Scott Key Elementary/Middle School, which was built in 1985 replacing a former school that fronted Fort Avenue. The GreMar Café building, just past the school, is another former movie theater.

6

Continue on Fort Avenue past Hull Street.

The Charles L. Stevens Funeral Home occupies three rowhouses that were once 1501 through 1505 East Fort Avenue. It was started in the 1920s, and is one of the oldest family-owned businesses on Locust Point. The funeral home originally occupied just the two outside units. For decades, the middle unit remained a private residence. It wasn't until about ten years ago that 1503 became incorporated into the funeral home.

Latrobe Park stands just past Latrobe Park Terrace. It was named for architect Benjamin Latrobe, who designed the Basilica of the Assumption in the Mt. Vernon neighborhood of Baltimore, and the United States Capitol building in Washington, D.C. The park serves as the center of recreational activity in Locust Point, but played an even greater role a century ago. It was once the site of a bathing beach. The Patapsco River used to lap up to the south face of Latrobe Park. A large bathhouse for the swimmers was located here. Construction of I-95 and the railroad tracks eliminated the beach. Notice the locust trees along some of the walkways in Latrobe Park. These are thought to be how Locust Point got its name.

A string of rowhouses along the west face of Latrobe Park is called Latrobe Park Terrace. Many of the original homes here were destroyed by a tornado in 1917, and had to be rebuilt.

Directly across from Latrobe Park is the Our Lady of Good Counsel Church. This was originally an Irish church established in the late nineteenth century. A statue of St. Lawrence O'Toole stands in front of the library beside the church. Its congregation in the mid-nineteenth century was led by Reverend James Gibbons (later Cardinal Gibbons) who was also pastor of a church in Canton. Priscilla Miles, in her book of walking tours titled *Historic Baltimore*, tells how he was able to handle both positions with the help of a rowboat that he anchored on a pier at the foot of Hull Street. He would travel back and forth across the harbor each day, tending to one church, and then the next. Reverend Gibbons was the spoken voice of many immigrants who settled here, as he strove to improve their labor situations.

Just past Latrobe Park, Fort Avenue crosses over the massive railroad yards still serving the port of Baltimore. Many cargo cranes bordering both sides of Fort Avenue make up the Locust Point Marine Terminal. Cross the bridge over the railroad yard, and note the white ship to the left. This is a former hospital ship that is being converted to a homeless shelter. The stack of massive grain silos to the left of the ship supplied tons of wheat to be shipped to the former Soviet

Union. Along the right side of Fort Avenue is where the Columbian Iron Works shipyard once operated. Many gunboats were built there for use in the Spanish-American War, as was the world-famous *Argonaut* submarine.

7

Enter through the gate of Fort McHenry (if open). Immediately turn right onto a paved walking path. Continue on the walking path for about one mile, circling the fort counter-clockwise.

As a public park, Fort McHenry is the perfect locale to soak up an afternoon while watching ships come in and out of the harbor. But the fort is better known for its invincible stand against the British in the War of 1812. Fort McHenry operated as a military installation beginning in the late 1700s, when the peninusla tip was called Whetstone Point, named for the mineral deposits found there. In 1794, Congress passed legislation to provide funding for a number of forts from Georgia through New England to protect the country's ports and harbors. Sixteen forts in all were built through this legislation, one of them Fort McHenry. Fort McHenry may be the finest surviving of the sixteen. People often mistake Fort McHenry for a star-shaped fort, which was a popular design during the revolution. In fact, it's a pentagonal-shaped structure with a bastion extending from each of its five corners.

Fort McHenry was involved in many battles. It gained its notoriety, however, by defending Baltimore against British attack during the War of 1812. The war was fought to preserve "free trade and Sailors' rights." British ships were impounding American vessels and attempting to control trade in and out of Baltimore's port. War was declared. The British navy routed Washington, D.C., and then unleashed a furious twenty-five-hour barrage on Baltimore's shore. Almost two thousand mortar shells buffeted Fort McHenry, and a massive land attack was attempted. Surprisingly, the soldiers serving Fort McHenry and the other ramparts about the waterfront rebuffed the attack. When the sun rose on the

The Argonaut

Simon Lake is considered the father of the modern submarine. In 1897, he successfully tested a privately funded submarine prototype, beating several heavily funded naval experiments to the punch. Lake's submersible was called the *Argonaut*, and was built at the former site of the Columbian Iron Works plant, once located near the present-day entrance gates to Fort McHenry. The *Argonaut*'s maiden voyage was off the tip of Fort McHenry. It was thirty-six feet long and ran on thirty horsepower. It could stay underwater for ten hours. Many features of modern submarines were derived from the *Argonaut*, including the use of ballast water to submerge, and an internal chamber where divers could go in and out. Though the primary purpose of the *Argonaut* was to provide assistance with marine salvage operations, its military implications were far reaching. In *Baltimore Harbor: A Picture History*, Robert C. Keith speculates that the launching of the *Argonaut* may have had greater long-term military significance than the defense of Fort McHenry.

second day of the attack and the maelstrom had calmed, British ships were seen fleeing the harbor. Soldiers at Fort McHenry hoisted a forty-two-by-thirty-foot flag and sang "Yankee Doodle." That banner now resides at the Smithsonian Institution's National Museum of American History, in Washington, D.C.

It was during this battle that Francis Scott Key penned the words to our national anthem, "The Star-Spangled Banner." In his book *Fort McHenry*, historian Scott Sheads notes that Key, a young local lawyer, was aboard a British truce ship during the invasion, just beyond where the Francis Scott Key Memorial Bridge now stands. He was negotiating a prisoner exchange. When the battle smoke cleared, Key, back on board the American sloop, could see the American flag flapping over the fort, and was so moved that he wrote the lyrics. Key's lyrics were set to the tune of "To Anacreon in Heaven," an English drinking song.

The legacy of Fort McHenry continued through subsequent wars. It served as a detention center for holding Confederate prisoners during the Civil War. During World

War I, it served as a massive hospital. Medical facilities were spread across the grounds in over one hundred makeshift wood-frame and cinder-block buildings. It could handle 3,000 patients and employed over 1,000 medical staff. The hospital only operated for seven years, and most of the medical buildings were removed soon after. In 1925, Fort McHenry became a national park.

The walk around Fort McHenry is one of Baltimore's finest. After turning right onto the walking path, look for the bronze statue hiding in the trees. It's of Orpheus, the Greek mythological hero of poetry and music. The statue originally graced the fort's entrance, but was moved to its present perch because some felt it diverted attention away from the military aspects of the fort.

Where the walking path first meets the water was one of Baltimore's most popular bathing beaches. It opened in 1915, when the fort retired from military duty and was bequeathed to the city for use as a public park. This bathing area was the first in the city where male and female bathers shared the same waters (though they were separated by a rope). About 1,000 bathers came here daily, each paying five cents for the privilege. Two years after its opening, however, the park shut down and the fort was returned to its military obligation.

Walking along the waterfront, notice the industrial areas across the Patapsco River. The area directly across is Fairfield, home to an assortment of shipbuilding and shipping piers. It was here that the world's first container ship was built, on the grounds of the Maryland Shipbuilding and Drydock Corporation. A large cylindrical water tower can be seen high on the hill. This is located in the residential neighborhood of Brooklyn. Farther along the walking path, look back for a view of Harbor Hospital, the starting point of this hike. Beyond the hospital is the neighborhood of Cherry Hill.

Near the tip of Fort McHenry, notice the lone Sycamore tree standing on the waterfront. This tree was once struck by lightning. The main trunk has been split in two, and charred remains can be seen inside the split.

Pause along the seawall where the first set of cannons face the water. There are three ways to cross the Patapsco

River by car. The first is on I-695 via the Francis Scott Key Memorial Bridge, which is visible in the distance. The second is on I-95 via the Fort McHenry Tunnel. This tunnel lies a few feet off the tip of Fort McHenry, and about fifty feet down. It was completed in 1985 at a cost of $825 million. The tunnel section in the main channel had to allow fifty feet of clearance overhead for the safe passage of ships. The third route across the Patapsco River is on I-895, via the Baltimore Harbor Tunnel. This lies beneath the river just beyond the Fort McHenry Tunnel.

8

Continue walking on the paved footpath along the seawall.

Several large silos emblazoned with "Lehigh Cement" stand across the Patapsco River. This area is the industrial part of Canton. The silos stand on Lazaretto Point. Lazaretto means "fever hospital" or "pesthouse" in Italian. This was the site of a large quarantine station for smallpox, which was built in 1801. Notice the piles of salt in the foreground, and coal to the rear.

A black Coast Guard tower stands along the Fort McHenry waterfront just past the tip. It is in direct line with the Patapsco River's primary shipping channel into Baltimore's harbor. Ships entering the harbor still count on this tower for guidance. Notice that the green beacon on the tower flashes every two seconds.

9

The paved walking path dead-ends in Fort McHenry's park-ing lot. Turn left onto the sidewalk. Follow the sidewalk to the fort's entrance gate.

Near the fort gate, note the brick building to the right and down the hill, the Naval Reserve Center, which holds great historical significance. This is where immigrants enter-ing Locust Point were processed beginning in 1916. Baltimore was one of the most prolific entry points into the United States. For example, in 1839, fifty-seven vessels of immigrants cleared Baltimore; by comparison, only thirty-eight passed through New York. Many immigrants at that time were coming into Henderson's Wharf, near Fells Point. As time progressed, the wharf could not handle the heavy traffic, and a new port had to be found. The B&O Railroad Company volunteered this pier, and Locust Point's first shipload of immigrants in 1868 entered to a cheering crowd and gun salute. It did not take long for Locust Point to become Baltimore's—and for a time, the nation's—premier point of entry. The Naval Reserve Center yard is also where much of the liquor confiscated in Baltimore during Prohibition was destroyed.

10

Exit Fort McHenry.
Continue on Fort Avenue through Locust Point.

Just past the bridge to the right stands a large concrete footprint of a former building, once the site of a brick B&O Railroad Company warehouse, which burned to the ground in the mid-1990s. It was a massive structure historically used to store tobacco. The warehouse was being targeted as a potential site for a neighborhood museum commemorating the many immigrants who passed through here. The warehouse was built on what was called Limey Field, where local soccer squads played teams of visiting English sailors.

11

Just past the bridge, turn right onto Andre Street.
Continue on Andre Street for two blocks.

This is the residential section of Locust Point. It's where thousands of immigrants who found work on the port or in the nearby factories settled. Many of these homes have always been privately owned rather than rented, since home ownership was vital to the immigrants. On the corner of Clement and Andre streets is J. Patrick's Restaurant and Tavern, one of Baltimore's genuine Irish pubs.

The brick and white-vinyl-sided building on the southeast corner of Beason and Andre streets was a former hotel owned by the B&O Railroad Company for its employees. Across Beason Street from the hotel are the former offices of the Southern States Company. This brick building contained the super-computer that controlled the colossal grain silos to the right.

12

**Turn left onto Beason Street.
Continue on Beason Street for five blocks.**

The Cuba Copper Smelting Company stood along the waterfront near here. Look for the gray brick building standing behind a series of garages near the corner of Towson and Beason streets. This was the first church established on Locust Point— an Episcopalian church built in 1855 by the Cuba Copper Smelting Company to serve its employees. Across Towson Street is the former Locust Point branch of

The Kings of Urban Renaissance

Baltimore should raise a glass to William and Fred Struever, Cobber Eccles, and Ted Rouse. The four are principal executives in Baltimore's most altruistic contracting firm—Struever Brothers, Eccles, and Rouse, Inc. William Struever and Eccles were classmates at Brown University in the 1970s. Struever graduated in 1973, earning a degree in Urban Studies, with a keen interest in urban restoration. His friend and classmate, Cobber Eccles, had a strong interest in historic renovation. They teamed up with William's brother Fred to form the original firm (sans Rouse, who joined the firm in 1984). The company's philosophy is that a city's neighborhood is not inviting without an established retail district nearby. The developers undertook their first renovations in Federal Hill, helping to convert it into one of Baltimore's most livable communities. They went on to develop parts of the city's most gentrified communities, including Tindeco Wharf and The Can Company in Canton. Struever Brothers, Eccles, and Rouse, Inc., also provide a substantial amount of charitable work to needy Baltimore entities. The Struever brothers' tenure in Baltimore has special significance: distant ancestors settled in Baltimore in the 1700s and owned businesses around the Inner Harbor.

the Enoch Pratt Free Library, now occupied by the shipping company Perishable Deliveries.

Beason Street crosses over Hull Street. Hull Street was a former commercial hub of Locust Point. It was named for Captain Isaac Hull, who guided the *USS Constellation* through the War of 1812. At the northern terminus of Hull Street is the former Procter & Gamble plant, where household products like Dawn, Joy, Tide, and Ivory were once manufactured. Procter & Gamble left town recently, and the plant has been converted to Tide Point Waterfront Park by Struever Brothers, Eccles, and Rouse, Inc. The Hull Street Blues Café is located to the right, at 1222 Hull Street. It's the building with three flags on its facade. This café is one of Locust Point's most popular hangouts, and home to one of Baltimore's favorite Sunday brunches. Hull Street Blues Café is one place to bring out-of-town guests wanting to experience "Baltimore" dining.

Next to the former Procter & Gamble plant is the massive Domino Sugar plant. Domino Sugar opened in 1922 as the largest and most modern sugar-processing plant in the world. Ships carrying the raw brown sugar from the Caribbean, Central, and South America are a common sight at its port.

13

Turn left onto Decatur Street.
Continue on Decatur Street for two blocks.

The Christ United Church of Christ, built in 1887, stands at the corner of Beason and Decatur streets. To local residents, it's simply known as the German Church. Notice the German lettering above the main entrance. The Immigration House building, built in 1904, stands next to the church. This is where transitional social services were provided to immigrants entering Locust Point.

The 1400 block of Decatur Street was home to the "Decatur Street Boys." This was the name given to the forty men (and boys) from this block who served at the same time during World War II.

14
Turn right onto Fort Avenue.
Continue on Fort Avenue for about four blocks.

15
Turn right onto Lawrence Street.
Continue on Lawrence Street for one block.

16
Turn left onto Key Highway.
Continue on Key Highway for about one-half mile.

The waterfront along Key Highway is one in transition. Maritime industries and weatherbeaten warehouses are giving way to restaurants and condominiums. The Downtown Sailing Center, a community sailing organization, is located at the foot of Lawrence Street. Just beyond it, occupying a three-story red brick building and green warehouse, is the Baltimore Museum of Industry. The museum occupies a nineteenth-century oyster cannery, and is said to be dedicated to the "Art of Work." The museum features hands-on exhibits of the city's industrial metamorphosis, making it equally popular with kids and adults. Featured displays involve canning, printing, and steelmaking. A new permanent exhibit highlights the garment industry, which at one time employed almost one-quarter of working Baltimoreans.

Just past the Museum of Industry is the shop where city fire trucks are maintained and repaired. Across the street, at 1414 Key Highway, is the South Harbor Business Center. This was once a pancake syrup manufacturing plant.

At the first bend in Key Highway sprawls the development known as Harborview, which includes townhouses, a marina, and a high-rise condominium. The high-rise was built to loosely resemble a lighthouse, and is set in sharp relief to the diminutive rowhouses of the adjoining neighborhood. This creative design did not appease some nearby Federal Hill residents who lost their waterfront view to the monolith. Harborview was built on the former dry docks of the

Bethlehem Steel Corporation, which conducted much of its ship-repair business here. The dry docks were active until the late 1980s. It was quite a sight to drive along Key Highway and see the massive vessels under repair lining the shoreline. The Harborview high-rise is constructed in one of these dry docks.

The Maine Lake Ice Company was once located near the Harborview development. Its main business was to bring refrigeration to Baltimore residents in the form of ice (before the age of electricity). Ice was cut from the Kennebec River and other Maine waterways, and brought to Baltimore aboard large schooners. (The schooners returned to Maine loaded with mid-Atlantic coal.) Ice blocks were unloaded into warehouses along Key Highway, and insulated with sawdust and straw. From there, they were dispensed to neighborhood homes via horse-drawn carts. Today, this area is home to Federal Hill's burgeoning antique market.

17

In front of the Harborview high-rise, turn left onto Cross Street. Continue on Cross Street for two blocks.

The church at 454 East Cross Street is the Sailor's Union Bethel Methodist Church. The church began in a ship in Baltimore's harbor in 1846. When the ship was condemned, the congregation—many of them visiting sailors—moved inland and settled in this building in 1873. The large building across from the church is Southern High School.

18

Turn right onto Riverside Avenue. Continue on Riverside Avenue for two blocks.

For years, Pfefferkorn's Coffee, Inc., roasted beans in a converted garage at the northeast corner of Grindall Street and Riverside Avenue, which provided a pleasant aroma to the neighborhood. The factory recently moved to a Locust Point warehouse.

19

Turn right onto Hamburg Street. Continue on Hamburg Street for two blocks, until it dead-ends.

At 337 East Hamburg Street was the headquarters of Union Civil War General Benjamin Butler while his troops were stationed on Federal Hill. Confederate spies were held prisoner in the basement, and some were executed in the front yard. Basement shackles were found in a renovation.

20

At the end of Hamburg Street, turn left onto a pathway leading to Federal Hill Park. Continue one block to the park. Walk around the face of the park.

For a detailed discussion of Federal Hill and the sights seen from the park, see the Waterfront Hike.

21

At the northwest corner of the park, descend the 100 steps to Battery Avenue. Continue across Battery Avenue, onto Montgomery Street. Continue on Montgomery Street for two blocks.

The colorful road surface material of Battery Avenue is called glasphalt—a combination of asphalt, slag, limestone powder, and glass. It was the idea of then city council president William Donald Schaefer, who thought it would help alleviate the city's solid-waste build-up. It proved expensive, and only a few streets in Baltimore possess this road treatment. Battery Avenue is so named because it leads to Riverside Park, which served as a military battery during the War of 1812.

Montgomery Street is one of the most coveted addresses in the city. The first six units to the left are referred to as the incomplete row. It is thought that the dwellings are set back from the street because they are only partially completed. Likely, the builders erected the functional areas—kitchen and bedrooms—hoping to come back and complete the parlor and

---

Fireman Follies

Fire companies in Baltimore city did not always set a stellar example of unity and sportsmanship. In his book *Federal Hill*, Norman G. Rukert tells how in the nineteenth century, fire companies routinely competed against one another—often in a violent manner. It was not unusual to see two competing fire companies engaged in a brawl while behind them a building was being swallowed by flames. Some fire companies would deliberately set fire to a building in another company's territory, and then ambush that company with a flurry of cobblestone as they headed to the blaze. Teenagers at that time often declared allegiance to one particular fire company, and would engage in scuffles with those affiliated with other companies. One particularly violent argument between fire companies happened in 1857 on Federal Hill, probably between the Watchman Fire Company and its nearby rival, the United States Hose Company. Several firemen were shot and a hose wagon ended up in the harbor.

---

public areas when money became available. It evidently never happened. Today the houses are blessed with front yards—a rarity in Federal Hill. The gentrification of Montgomery Street did not begin in earnest until the 1970s. At that time, the asphalt was pulled up from the street—by the local residents, not the city—exposing the original cobblestone.

Rowhouses are narrow by nature, but 200½ East Montgomery Street might be the skinniest in the city, measuring about eighty-seven inches wide. At 130 East Montgomery Street is a rare wooden rowhouse that was built before wooden rowhouses were outlawed in the city (for fear of fire); and at 125 East Montgomery Street is the former Watchman Fire Company Building, which now serves as a private residence. The building was erected in 1843, soon after the fire company was incorporated by an act of legislature.

22
Turn left onto Light Street.
Continue on Light Street for five blocks.

Look left down Churchill Street, one of Federal Hill's many alley streets. The narrowness and uniqueness of this attractive byway has a European flair. Some of the tiny houses along Churchill Street were converted from warehouses and garages.

The Light Street Presbyterian Church stands along Light Street between Montgomery and Churchill streets. Many German and English immigrants settled in the Federal Hill section of the city, and their first concern was to establish places of worship. Light Street Presbyterian Church was one of the first built, being completed in 1855. It was formerly called the South Church.

Light Street is lined with busy shops and eateries including Sam's Bagels, Ten-O-Six, and Blue Agave Restaurante. Across from the South Baltimore Recreation Center is the former McHenry Theater, now occupied by a restaurant. Notice its name near the building's roofline. Plans occasionally surface to convert this structure to a parking garage to alleviate the weekend parking congestion in Federal Hill.

23

**Turn right into Cross Street Market.
Continue to the opposite end of the market.
[Alternatively, turn right onto Cross Street, just
before the market, and continue for one block.]**

Cross Street Market has been in existence since 1846, and has been at this location since 1873. It's one of the seven city-run public farmers' markets operating in Baltimore. The present building dates to 1952, after a fire leveled the previous structure. Not only is Cross Street Market the ideal place to buy produce, flowers, and specialty foods, but the west end of the market, around Nick's Inner Harbour Seafood, features one of Baltimore's most popular happy hours.

24

**Turn left onto Charles Street. Continue on Charles Street
for about one-half mile, until Wells Street.**

Charles Street holds a large number of Federal Hill's favorite shops and cafés. Two of the most popular are Mother's Federal Hill Grille and Vespas, located just after

Cross Street Market. These two cafés occupy what was once Muhly's Bakery. This business establishment supplied South Baltimore residents with breads and sweets from 1852 through the early 1990s. Eberhardt Muhly was a German carpenter who built an oven in his backyard at 1115 South Charles Street. He fueled it with scraps of wood left over from his woodworking business. Besides baking his own bread, Muhly allowed neighbors to bring dough, which he would bake for two pennies each. Five years later, Muhly laid down his hammer for good, becoming a full-time baker.

25

**Turn right onto Wells Street.
Continue on Wells Street for one block.**

26

**Turn left onto Hanover Street. Continue on Hanover Street across the Vietnam Veterans Memorial Bridge.
Stay left across the bridge.**

27

Just across the Vietnam Veterans Memorial Bridge, turn left into the public parking lot of Broening Park. The hike ends in this parking lot.

Suggested Reading

Books

Federal Hill by Norman G. Rukert

Baltimore Harbor: A Picture History by Robert C. Keith

Fort McHenry by Scott Sheads

Historic Baltimore: Twelve Walking Tours of Downtown, Fells Point, Locust Point, Federal Hill, and Mount Clare by Priscilla L. Miles

Wish You Were Here! A Guide to Baltimore City for Natives and Newcomers by Carolyn Males, Carol Barbier Rolnick, and Pam Makowski Goresh

Baltimore: The Building of an American City by Sherry H. Olson

Websites

Fort McHenry National Monument
www.nps.gov/fomc

Baltimore City Government
www.ci.baltimore.md.us

Baltimore Area and Visitors Association
www.baltconvstr.com

Welcome to South Baltimore
www.southbaltimore.com

Port of Baltimore
www.mpa.state.md.us

Live Baltimore Home Center
www.livebaltimore.com

East Baltimore

Pagoda in Patterson Park

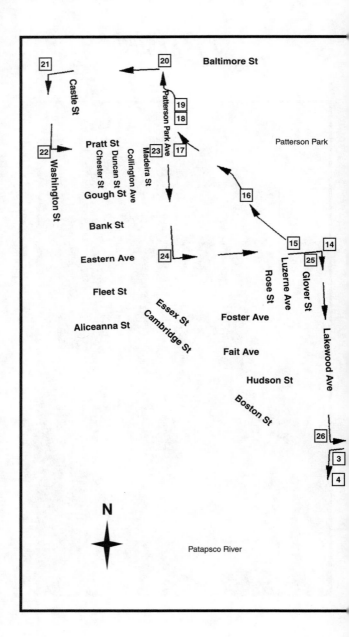

Overview

Distance: Five miles.

Major attractions: The neighborhoods of Canton, Highlandtown, and Butchers Hill; and Patterson Park.

Starting location: O'Donnell Square, which is located on O'Donnell Street between Potomac Street and Linwood Avenue.

Directions to start and parking: From downtown Baltimore, take Pratt Street east. Continue on Pratt Street for about one mile past President Street, until it dead-ends at Patterson Park. Turn right onto Patterson Park Avenue. Continue on Patterson Park Avenue for three blocks. Turn left at the light onto Eastern Avenue. Continue east on Eastern Avenue along the southern boundary of Patterson Park. At the third light, turn right onto Linwood Avenue. Continue on Linwood Avenue for six blocks, until it meets O'Donnell Square. Free on-street parking is usually available on or near the square.

From I-95, take Exit 59, Eastern Avenue, west toward downtown Baltimore. Continue on Eastern Avenue, through the Highlandtown business district, to Patterson Park. Turn left onto Linwood Avenue, which is the first light past Ellwood Avenue. Continue on Linwood Avenue for six blocks, until it meets O'Donnell Square. Free on-street parking is usually available on or near the square.

Access to eating facilities: O'Donnell Square offers a wide selection of restaurants and pubs. Additional eateries can be found along Eastern Avenue in Highlandtown.

Introduction

Canton epitomizes recent gentrification of Baltimore's formerly industrial neighborhoods. BMWs zip down Boston Street, where only eighteen-wheelers once roamed. Smokestacks that until recently billowed smoke are now merely ornamentation to luxurious condos converted from factories. Refurbished pint-sized rowhouses now command six-figure price tags. The new Canton is a clean, crisp twenty-something nirvana, and the city's testament to change. Right next door is Highlandtown, a sea of rolling rowhouses that has resisted change and retained its old-Baltimore charm. Marble steps here are still scrubbed by hand and the word "Hon" is frequently bandied about. And along the way lies Butchers Hill, where the old and the new converge. Gentrification is ongoing, but not yet complete. This hike will travel through all three neighborhoods, providing insight into what's new in Baltimore, what's old, and what's changing.

1

Begin the hike at the John O'Donnell statue in O'Donnell Square.

O'Donnell Square lies along O'Donnell Street, between Potomac Street and Linwood Avenue. The square is the former location of a large farmers' market pavilion that served the surrounding neighborhoods. Today, it's a manicured park, with brick pathways and benches, surrounded by trendy pubs, cafés, and specialty shops.

The statue in the square's center is of Canton's founder, Captain John O'Donnell. In 1785, O'Donnell arrived in Baltimore aboard his ship, the *Pallas*, and settled on an estate of about 2,000 acres along the north shore of the Patapsco River. There, he grew peaches that he turned into a popular brandy, and continued to amass great wealth from his merchant business. The neighborhood of Canton is situated on O'Donnell's former estate. O'Donnell died here at the age of 56. He was one of the wealthiest men in the country at the time.

Messiah English Lutheran Church is the gray stone chapel on the east end of O'Donnell Square. The church was built in 1889 using granite quarried from around Port Deposit, Maryland, in Cecil County about forty miles away. Immediately behind Messiah English Lutheran Church, and facing Ellwood Avenue, is the Canton branch of the Enoch Pratt Free Library. This is one of four original libraries built by philanthropist Enoch Pratt, and the only one still in use as a library. It was completed in 1886.

2

Walk west on O'Donnell Street toward the Engine No. 22 firehouse. Pass to the right of the firehouse, and continue on O'Donnell Street for two blocks, until it dead-ends at the Safeway market.

Crossing Kenwood Avenue, look right. In a former time, locals gave rowhouse blocks nicknames. "Brick Row," for example, is on the right side of Kenwood Avenue, extending from O'Donnell Street to Dillon Street. The four units closest

---

What's in a name?

The source of Canton's name may appear obvious. After all, the Canton waterfront was home to dozens of canneries, where oysters and produce were packaged in tins. Other nearby factories produced the cans used in the canneries, and others decorated the tins. The entire area was referred to as "Cannery Row." But the name of the Canton neighborhood has nothing to do with the canning industry. Rather, it takes its name from the port city of Canton (now Guangzhou), in south China. When Captain John O'Donnell arrived in Baltimore aboard the *Pallas*, he was carrying a cargo load of silks, spices, crafted items, and teas from Canton, China, which was his favorite destination. He sold his wares to Baltimoreans, becoming quite wealthy. O'Donnell bought his estate, named it Canton in honor of the Chinese port city, and spent his remaining years here. Before his death at age 56, O'Donnell made one final voyage to Asia, where his ship, the *Chesapeake*, was the first American ship to trade with India, and the first to fly the American flag on the Ganges River.

to Dillon Street are one of the oldest intact rows in Baltimore.

St. Casmir's Church is the stately twin-towered chapel, just past the firehouse. St. Casmir's Church is named for a wealthy Polish prince, and is the culmination of Father Ben Przemielewski's dream of building in Baltimore a Renaissance-style church with an altar replicating that of the Basilica of St. Anthony in Padua, Italy. The church was erected in 1926 to serve Canton's burgeoning Polish population. It is constructed of Indiana limestone. Notice the hand-carved wooden doors and statues of Saint Francis of Assisi and Saint Anthony of Padua on the towers. The church's interior is covered with moving Renaissance-style murals, and is worth a peek.

3

Turn left onto Lakewood Avenue. Continue on Lakewood Avenue for one block, until it dead-ends on Boston Street.

Before crossing Boston Street, look right. This area was once called "Cannery Row," named for the many canneries that lined the waterfront. Chesapeake oysters, eastern shore vegetables, and other products were canned here and exported from the port. This area of Boston Street is now referred to as the "Gold Coast" for its newfound concentration of wealth. Boston Street was named in deference to the many New Englanders who settled here to work in the canneries.

Anchorage Towers is the tall residential structure on the waterfront to the right. Beyond the tower is a string of forty-eight townhouses facing the waterfront marina, the conception of then-Mayor William Donald Schaefer, who saw a similar housing arrangement while visiting Boston. They were built in 1982. The Anchorage development was built in 1982 as the first substantial residential waterfront development in the refurbished Canton.

Across the street and just beyond the Anchorage development is the former American Can Company building, which was saved from demolition by the development firm of Struever Brothers, Eccles, and Rouse, Inc. An early refurbishment plan had the factory being razed and replaced with two twenty-seven-story, glass-and-metal condominium and business towers. That idea was squelched, and the factory was instead converted to shops and high-tech businesses.

Just before Anchorage Towers, Harris Creek flows into the harbor from a culvert beneath the streets. Along these banks of the harbor is where Major John Stodder opened a boatyard centuries ago. In 1797, he built and launched from here the *Constellation*, whose namesake ship is now an inner harbor tourist attraction. The ship is thought to have been built using slave labor.

4

Cross over Boston Street and turn left.
Continue on Boston Street for one block.

The modern rowhouse development to the left is Canton Square. Plans surfaced in the 1960s to build a six-lane expressway through Federal Hill, Fells Point, and Canton. The highway project would have extended the Jones Falls Expressway to I-95, to the detriment of the character of miles of waterfront. Hundreds of rowhouses were demolished in preparation. Community activists—most notably future U.S. Senator Barbara Mikulski—were able to halt the planned highway, and the present Canton Square development was built to replace the lost houses. This battle launched Mikulski's distinguished political career.

Across from Canton Square is the J.S. Young Company building, which is now occupied by, among other stores, Blockbuster and West Marine. The J.S. Young Company manufactured licorice to flavor the tobacco grown in outlying regions, and also produced dyes and tanning extracts. Notice the company's name set in yellow brick on the structure's side.

Just beyond the J.S. Young Company is Tindeco Wharf, a trendy apartment complex easily identifiable by its two red-capped water towers on the roof. Tindeco Wharf is the reincarnation of the Tin Decorating Company, once the largest and finest tin lithography plant in the world. It opened for business in 1914, and quickly grew to employ 3,000 workers churning out millions of tin boxes. The company initially produced tins for the American Tobacco Company, but soon expanded its repertoire to include decorative containers for cakes, cookies, medicine, talcum, and candy. The factory was unusual in that it had its own hospital. Said one employee, "If you were working in a tin factory on a production line, and still had all your fingers, you were lucky." Behind Tindeco Wharf, on the waterfront, is the Bay Café, whose building used to be the powerhouse for the decorating plant. It's now a festive indoor-outdoor eatery.

5

Just before Tindeco Wharf, walk through the parking lot to the waterfront. Turn left just past the apartment building. Pass between the manufacturing plant and the Bay Café restaurant. Continue along the brick promenade.

The brick promenade is part of a grand plan to make Baltimore's waterfront accessible to pedestrians. When complete, it will wrap continuously around the inner harbor from Fort McHenry to Canton, a distance of over seven miles.

Just beyond Tindeco Wharf is the Canton Cove Condominium. The structure was also a tin decorating plant, this one for the American Can Company. It's where containers for such products as Coca-Cola and Lucky Strikes were fabricated.

6

Continue on the brick promenade for one block, until Canton Cove Park.

Canton Cove Park provides tranquil respite to busy Canton. In 1893, this waterfront became the first public bathing beach in Baltimore (indoor plumbing was non-existent at that time). It was also referred to as the Baptizing Shore, being used by the emerging neighborhood Baptist church congregations for ceremonies. The bay just off

Canton Cove Park is where centuries ago the armada of Baltimore clipper ships moored after returning from Brazil with mounds of coffee beans. Today, the park affords sweeping views of Fort McHenry across the bay, and Canton's industrial waterfront to the left, lined with refineries, smelting plants, shipping operations, and various other manufacturing plants.

7

Enter Canton Cove Park and walk left toward the pair of flagpoles.

The Korean Veterans Memorial is bounded by two flagpoles, one bearing the United States flag, and the other the Maryland and POW-MIA flags. A map of the Korean War theater is incised in stone on the ground, and a low wall to the north names all 525 Marylanders who lost their lives there. A south wall details battles of the war. A string of brick inlaid on the etched stone connecting the two flagpoles represents the 38th parallel.

8

From the Korean Veterans Memorial, turn right onto Boston Street. Continue on Boston Street for two blocks.

To the left is the Clarence H. "Du" Burns Arena built in 1990 as a multi-functional recreational facility. It's used primarily for indoor soccer and lacrosse. Burns, from East Baltimore, was the first black mayor of Baltimore, serving just after William Donald Schaefer.

9

Turn left onto Clinton Street. Continue on Clinton Street for three blocks.

The Canton Race Track once stood on the corner of Boston and Clinton streets. In the nineteenth century, revelers from downtown Baltimore flocked here on weekends by steamboat to drink and gamble on the horses. It was at the Canton Race Track that, in 1840, 20,000 Whigs from across the nation assembled to nominate William Henry Harrison as their presidential candidate. This is generally considered to have been the first presidential nominating convention in the United States.

Turn left onto Clinton Street, and notice the former Atlantic-Southwestern Broom Company building across the field to the right. This now houses artists' studios and other businesses. Along Clinton Street is the start of the seemingly endless rowhouse communities of East Baltimore. This is where waves of immigrants—among them Polish, German, Irish, and Ukranian—settled beginning centuries ago. The signature features of East Baltimore rowhouses are the marble stoops, stained glass transoms, and the occasional painted window screen. As you traverse the neighborhood, pay particular attention to these details.

The first block of houses on Clinton Street to the right (numbers 1301 through 1313) reflect the hodgepodge of construction and upkeep of houses. Here, some units are three stories, and others two. Some retained their brick facades,

---

Painted window screens

In the Baltimore guidebook *Wish You Were Here!*, Carolyn Males, Carol Barbier Rolnick, and Pam Makowski Goresh provide a history of the Baltimore tradition of screenpainting. According to the authors, the practice took root in Newark, New Jersey. In 1912, secretaries in a manufacturing plant there complained of pedestrians peering into their office windows. A fellow employee, William Oktavek, took a window screen home and painted on it a jardiniere of flowers and cream-colored draperies, making the screen opaque to outsiders. Oktavek later moved to Baltimore and opened a grocery store. Vegetables he placed outside quickly spoiled from the sun, so Oktavek placed the produce inside and painted a screen on the window to deflect the rays. A neighbor asked him to paint a screen for her front window to prevent "rubberneckers" from looking in. He painted for her a red mill scene, taken from a calendar picture. Soon after, Oktavek was inundated with orders. In one ten-week stretch, he painted 375 screens. Most have since disappeared. Today, painted window screens are making a revival in Baltimore City, thanks to a handful of artists set on keeping this tradition alive.

whereas others have been overlaid with formstone or siding. This disjointed construction is in stark contrast to the uniform rows found just ahead in Highlandtown. The cornice is the decorative horizontal feature running along the front roofline of the house, which throws water off the house and in some cases helps ventilate attics. Notice how some cornices on this row have been encapsulated in aluminum siding.

Cross over Elliott Street, and look right to learn why the knoll rising here was once called Lager Beer Hill. The brick warehouse three blocks away, with "Hamms" scrawled across the facade, is one of about a dozen former breweries that once pocked this neighborhood. Many East Baltimore residents slogged up Lager Beer Hill on weekends to the taverns that surrounded the breweries. At the corner of Clinton and Elliot streets, notice the former Canton National Bank building, which now is a private residence. This building is identifiable as a bank from the large replica concrete coins embedded near the roofline.

Just past Elliot Street, 1137 Clinton Street reflects a painted window screen on the lower floor. The picture on the screen is of a red mill, a typical East Baltimore composition.

10
Turn right onto O'Donnell Street. Continue on O'Donnell Street for three blocks.

11
Turn left onto Conkling Street. Continue on Conkling Street for six blocks.

The bold-faced brick edifice at the intersection of O'Donnell and Conkling streets was once the National Brewing Company, where National Bohemian, National Premium, and other beers were brewed beginning in the 1880s. This structure is being explored for possible development.

Walk along Conkling Street, and notice that the rowhouses become more orderly and uniform. This is the transition from Canton to Highlandtown. Look for an increase in the number of brightly colored stained-glass windows and marble stoops.

Formstone

Often the first question posed by visitors to Baltimore is, What's with the gray rock? Here's what you tell them. High-quality brick was used to build houses for a wealthy clientele, but inferior brick was incorporated into the working-class neighborhoods. The low-grade brick proved porous, and required frequent painting to prevent the seepage of rain. In the 1940s and 1950s, formstone was marketed as the savior for inferior-quality brick. Formstone is not just faux stone hammered to the brick, but is actually a stucco material that's spread and shaped by hand on the house's facade. The sales pitch was that formstone didn't need painting, provided energy-efficient insulation, was inexpensive, and looked quite spiffy. Baltimore not only bought the concept, but ran with it. To have formstone was to have arrived. Formstone molders draped the city in drab gray. Today the removal of formstone is the indicator of a neighborhood's gentrification.

Conkling Street, between Fait and Foster avenues, is a canyon of formstone. Formstone molders placed tiny plaques near the front stoop to identify their work. At 724 Conkling Street is a "Field of Ages" tag, and 720 bears an "Original Hand-Sculpted" tag. Notice the different colors, textures, and designs of the various brands of formstone. Baltimore film director John Waters called formstone the "polyester of brick." Immigrant homeowners boasted they felt as if they were living in stone fortresses.

On Foster Avenue, the Sacred Heart of Jesus Church sports an impressive and ornate facade. The church was built in 1908 on the former site of Fort Marshall. This fort was hastily slapped together in the days preceding the Civil War to protect Baltimore from attacks of the Southern army. It was used to guard Fort McHenry, immediately across the harbor. When the war ended, the fort became expendable, and the land was sold to the church. German was the original tongue spoken at the church. Just beyond the church, along Conkling Street, is a granite monument dedicated to those parishioners who served in World War II. Across from the church, notice the unique row of houses with porches and second-floor bays. These architectural elements are infrequently found in East Baltimore, but are more common in later rowhouse developments to the north of downtown.

Crossing Fleet Street, look right for a sweeping view of East Baltimore. The cluster of brick institutional buildings on the far hill is the Johns Hopkins Bayview Medical Center.

Besides its breweries—or because of them—Highlandtown was once home to a slew of movie theaters and saloons. The Deco shell of the Grand movie house, just before Eastern Avenue, is a memento to those golden years. The 3500 block of Eastern Avenue, just around the corner from the Grand, was once home to twenty-three beer halls. Highlandtown was originally an entity of Baltimore County. At that time, Baltimore city had blue laws, disallowing the sale of alcoholic beverages on Sundays. Highlandtown, being in the county and liberated from blue laws, became a favorite Sunday destination for swarms of city revelers seeking cheer. Highlandtown was annexed to the city in 1919.

12

Turn left onto Eastern Avenue. Continue on Eastern Avenue, through the Highlandtown business district.

Unlike many urban shopping districts, Eastern Avenue remains a beehive of activity. As you approach the Highland Street intersection, notice the Baltimore City skyline straight ahead. From this vantage, it's easy to see how Highlandtown got its name. The canopy of foliage at the bottom of the hill is Patterson Park.

One block past Highland Street is Clinton Street. On the far right corner stands what used to be Haussner's restaurant, widely considered to have been the consummate Baltimore eatery. Haussner's was founded in 1926 and closed it doors in 1999, depriving Baltimoreans of masterful German food and the city's best strawberry shortcake. Over time, the Haussner family amassed an impressive collection of paintings and statues, including works by Rembrandt and Whistler. They displayed them in their dining area. Sotheby's auction house called the display one of the best private nineteenth-century art collections in the country. Sotheby's auctioned off the artwork after the restaurant closed.

Just past East Avenue is the former Patterson Theater, which, as of 2003, became the Patterson Center for the Arts, a neighborhood cultural center focusing on theater and the arts. The center was opened by the Fells Point Creative Alliance. Across and farther along Eastern Avenue is Matthew's Pizzeria, which has been serving outstanding Italian food since 1943. The many "Best of Baltimore" awards across the front window attest to Matthew's reputation.

13

Continue on Eastern Avenue past Ellwood Avenue.

Patterson Park begins just past Ellwood Avenue. The 155-acre park is the former estate of merchant William Patterson, and was opened to the public in 1853. Patterson Park carries a rich history. In the early nineteenth century, waterfront residents retreated here in droves to escape the scourge of yellow fever. During the War of 1812, fortifications here fended off British attack. During the Civil War, the park harbored a temporary hospital for soldiers wounded at the Battle of Gettysburg.

Patterson Park today remains the wellspring of East Baltimore. Spread across the park is an ensemble of recreational facilities that include soccer, baseball, and football fields; an Olympic-size swimming pool; a hockey rink; a community center; and a 2.6-acre pond.

The rowhouse development to the left was the creation of Edward Gallagher, who emerged in the early 1900s as the most prolific builder around Patterson Park. His trademark dwellings were modest, mostly two stories. The area became known as Park Side. In his prime, Gallagher was building over 200 houses per year here. His houses incorporated extensive marble work and stained glass. The marble was extracted from the Beaver Dam quarry north of Baltimore, which is now a public swimming hole. It's said that the uniformity of the rowhouse fosters a community spirit, while accessories to each house express individuality.

Why was the rowhouse so popular in Baltimore? One reason is that it allowed working- and middle-class citizens to own a house that was essentially similar to the houses owned by the wealthy—only smaller. Rowhouses of the elite class featured ornate marble work, stained glass windows, entry parlors, and detailed cornices. So did the rowhouses of the lower classes, only to a lesser degree. Another reason for the rowhouse's popularity was its affordability, both to the builder and the buyer. A century ago, Baltimore had one of the highest rates of home ownership in the country, because of the low cost of the rowhouse and the emergence of building and loan organizations to promote financing.

Mary Ellen Hayward and Charles Belfoure explain the history of Gallagher's housebuilding around Patterson Park in *The Baltimore Rowhouse*. According to the authors, Gallagher developed four classifications of houses in Park Side. The most expensive had a full marble front around the basement, a marble stoop, a wide plate-glass front window topped with stained glass, and a stained glass transom above the door. Most of the houses facing Patterson Park along Eastern Avenue fit this mold.

Gallagher's second-tier houses had marble sills and steps, but only a marble stringer across the facade, replacing the full marble basement front. They also had stained glass transoms. The third-tier houses had marble steps and a marble stringer, but no stained glass. The fourth had no marble at all, and only wooden steps. The cost variation between the different tier houses was surprisingly minimal, since marble work and stained glass were relatively inexpensive at the time. Full marble on the facade cost about $65, and the stained glass for an upper-level house cost about $60.

Look left down Curley Street, which is three blocks past Ellwood Avenue. The houses along Curley Street are examples of Gallagher's second-tier houses, which have a thin marble stringer across the facade instead of a full marble front. Notice that most houses still have stained glass windows and marble stoops. Also notice that Curley Street was a less vital thoroughfare than Eastern Avenue, where the more expensive homes were built. As was typical of that era,

Gallagher built the upper-tier houses along the major routes, the middle-tier houses in the secondary streets and wider alley streets, and the lower-tier houses in the more narrow alley streets.

14

Continue on Eastern Avenue past Lakewood Avenue.

One block past Lakewood Avenue, look left down Glover Street. Here are examples of Gallagher's lower-tier houses, with no marble and only small, simple, stained-glass transoms.

15

Continue on Eastern Avenue for one block past Glover Street. Where Luzerne Avenue enters from the left, take a right into the park on the paved pathway. Walk toward the wrought-iron fence about 100 yards away. Stay to the left of the fence.

The wrought-iron fence encloses the Patterson Park pond, home to an annual fishing derby and an overwinter population of mallard and wood ducks. The mallards are most common. Males are grayish with a shiny green head, brown collar, and black tail. Wood ducks, though not necessarily rare, are an uncommon sight in Baltimore City. The male wood duck also has a green head, but is identifiable by its brown and rust body and interesting pattern of white streaks across its head. The females of both species are a nondescript brown. The waterfowl congregate around the willow tree on the pond's island, or in the reed thickets.

16

Stay left on the walking path toward the Pagoda. Just past the pond, turn left onto a brick pathway. The Pagoda should be about 100 yards to the right, and a pavilion just to the left.

17

Just before the brick pathway meets Patterson Park Avenue, turn right onto a paved pathway that runs alongside the avenue, but inside the park.

The Patterson Park Observatory, also known as the Pagoda, was designed by Charles Latrobe, and built in 1891. The sixty-foot-high octagonal structure was recently renovated and offers panoramic views of East Baltimore and the Chesapeake Bay. Notice the twin towers of St. Casmir's Church and the red-capped water towers atop the Tindeco Wharf apartments. Farther away, look for the Francis Scott Key Memorial Bridge crossing the Patapsco River. The five cannons beside the Pagoda were used to successfully stave off British offenses during the Battle of North Point, in 1814.

18

Continue on the pedestrian path alongside Patterson Park Avenue.

Just beyond the Pagoda, and near the stone fountain, is a gated entrance to Patterson Park. This was designed as the park's main entrance, being where Lombard Street, the city's primary east-west artery, meets the park. Look down Lombard Street for an attractive view of the Baltimore skyline. Even though Lombard Street was considered the main entrance to Patterson Park, the larger and more elaborate houses in this area were built along Baltimore and Pratt streets, where the streetcars ran. This implied that it was more desirable to live on a streetcar route than around the entrance to a grand park. Just beyond the fountain is the former house of the gatekeeper.

19

Exit Patterson Park through the stone gate by the fountain. Turn right onto Patterson Park Avenue. Continue on Patterson Park Avenue for one block.

This area is known as Butchers Hill, or what used to be called Hampstead Hill. The neighborhood is named for the dozens of butchers and slaughterhouses that sprang up here in the nineteenth century. In 1812, Baltimore passed an ordinance outlawing slaughterhouses in populated areas. About fifty butchers in Baltimore sought solace high on this hill, where their odiferous operations would not affect the communities below, and where cattle farms to the east were easily accessible. Butchers Hill may have been the first substantial Baltimore-area settlement not built on a watercourse.

During the Civil War, the butchers prospered, selling their meat to the troops stationed in Patterson Park. When the war ended, many found themselves quite wealthy, and able to afford respectable houses. Most houses in Butchers Hill date from 1850 through 1915, and are of grand quality and design. By the 1920s, the butchers moved on, their businesses displaced by wholesale meatpackers like Esskay, but many of their attractive houses remain. A Jewish influx followed, lasting a few decades. The neighborhood then fell into disrepair. The gentrification process began in 1982, when Butchers Hill was included in the National Register of Historic Places. Today, most of the refurbished houses remain loyal to their original designs.

20

Turn left onto Baltimore Street.
Continue on Baltimore Street for three blocks.

Historically, east-west streets were considered more desirable in Baltimore since they tended to be the busier streets that accommodated traffic flow in and out of the city. Accordingly, they usually harbored larger and more elaborate houses. Baltimore Street is such a thoroughfare. Most houses along the Butchers Hill section of Baltimore Street are three stories high, three bays wide, and have a substantial back lot. The first row on the left, 2201 through 2239 East Baltimore Street, contradicts the repetitiveness considered inherent in rowhouse development. Each house in the row has ample space, but a close inspection reveals an assortment of architectural styles and accessories. With their stylish brick facades, 2215 and 2217 East Baltimore Street were once a freestanding pair, but were later incorporated into the row. In 1874, 2207 East Baltimore Street was constructed as a saloon. It still reflects the intact storefront, unusual for a mid-row unit. At the far end of the block, notice the disjointed but interesting roofline.

Across East Baltimore Street, 2200 through 2216 were all built of similar design, so as to resemble a single architectural unit. Notice the tower on each end unit, giving the entire block the appearance of a fortress.

Just past where Collington Avenue enters from the left, look right up Duncan Street. Alley streets such as Duncan Street can be found throughout Butchers Hill, and were developed later to fill in the available space. Houses could be built in alley streets at a fraction of the cost of main-street houses. These hidden rows allowed the middle- and working-class to infiltrate the neighborhood.

One block up, 2115 and 2117 East Baltimore Street served as the Belmont Stables, where Butchers Hill residents without carriage houses could board their horses, and where buggies were available for rent. The faded painted signage for the stables is visible on the lower side wall of 2115.

Notice the arching doorways on 2101 through 2113 East Baltimore Street. Charles Blake built this row in 1876. Blake was an accomplished builder who designed fashionable rowhouses in downtown Baltimore. He brought many ornate "downtown" features to his Butchers Hill houses.

Perhaps the most impressive house in Butchers Hill is the Bankard-Gunther Mansion at 2102 East Baltimore Street. The house was built around 1866 for Joseph J. Bankard, one of the butchers who became quite wealthy during the Civil War. It was a freestanding house at that time. Notice the change in the colors of the brick between the mansion and the remaining row, which was added later. In the late nineteenth century, when butchers fled the hill, the mansion was bought by George Gunther, who owned a large brewery on Conkling Street. The mansion has since been carved into apartments. Notice the well-preserved carriage house with cupola behind the Bankard-Gunther Mansion, which is now a private residence.

21
Turn left onto Washington Street.
Continue on Washington Street for two blocks.

The north-south streets in Butchers Hill historically were considered less fashionable, and thus are lined with more modest two- and three-story houses. They tend to have shorter lots and be less ornate in design. However, while many of the grand rowhouses along the east-west thorough-fares have been subdivided into multi-family dwellings, the houses along the north-south routes and in the alley streets have generally remained single-family dwellings.

Just past Lombard Street, at 101 Washington Street, is the former Excelsior Cigar Factory, which was established in 1871 and now serves as a private residence. Notice the lettering high on its pediment that identifies its former function. Across the street, the second-story balcony of 1928 Washington Street reveals one of the few remaining examples of wrought-iron work, once popular throughout Butchers Hill.

Just before Pratt Street is an attractive wall mural. The freestanding gray house with red trim catercorner from the wall mural is the Weiskittel House. Built in the Italianate style around 1873, the house features a sprayed asbestos covering.

22
Turn left onto Pratt Street.
Continue on Pratt Street for three blocks.

The earliest freestanding home in Butchers Hill is the Gosnell-Ehrman House at 2019 East Pratt Street. It was built in the Greek Revival style around 1852. Unlike many other original freestanding houses, the Gosnell-Ehrman House stands alone today, though it blends nicely into its surrounding row. Lewis Ehrman, former occupant of the house, was a ship chandler with stores in Fells Point and Locust Point.

The one-story white stone building on the corner of Pratt and Charles streets was built in 1926 as a garage. It's the most recent commercial structure built in Butchers Hill, and now serves as office and retail space.

Notice the row at 2112 through 2124 East Pratt Street: 2112 through 2118 were built in 1869, and feature small carved cornices; 2120 through 2124 were built in 1880, and feature taller, more elaborate, bracketed cornices. Advances in jigsaws and wood-carving machinery over the eleven-year span allowed for more ornate cornices.

The Griffin House at 2200 East Pratt Street was another individually built house, this one dating to 1860. It has since been incorporated into a row. It was built for Thomas C. Griffin, a Fells Point attorney. Both built freestanding, 2214 and 2218 East Pratt Street remain so today. On the second floor of the house just past 2218, notice the elaborate iron work, which used to be a Butchers Hill trademark.

23

Turn right onto Patterson Park Avenue.
Continue on Patterson Park Avenue for three blocks.

The pair of houses at 206 and 208 Patterson Park Avenue was built around 1870, and is set back behind a wrought-iron fence; 206 has painted window screens on the basement windows. A peculiarity of this duplex is that each unit was built more narrow than its lot to accommodate side entrances.

24

Turn left onto Eastern Avenue.
Continue on Eastern Avenue for about nine short blocks.

The turnip-domed St. Michael the Archangel Ukrainian Catholic Church stands at the corner of Eastern and Montford avenues. The congregation opened this sanctuary in 1991 after moving from Wolfe Street in Fells Point. The building is constructed in the shape of a Greek cross. Services are given in both English and Ukrainian.

25

Turn right onto Lakewood Avenue. Continue on Lakewood
Avenue for six blocks, until the Safeway market.

Along Lakewood Avenue, notice how the rowhouses become plainer the farther from Patterson Park they are situated. Full marble stringer fronts and the second stained-glass window disappear from many houses by the 700 block. The marble steps vanish from most houses by the 800 block. At 940 Lakewood Avenue is the Indecco Apartment building, which was once the Independent Decorating Company. Fading advertisements still grace the exterior walls leading back to Cannery Row.

26

Turn left onto O'Donnell Street. Continue on O'Donnell Street for two blocks. The hike ends at O'Donnell Square.

Suggested Reading

Books

Wish You Were Here! A Guide to Baltimore City for Natives and Newcomers by Carolyn Males, Carol Barbier Rolnick, and Pam Makowski Goresh

Walking in Baltimore: An Intimate Guide to the Old City by Frank R. Shivers, Jr.

The Baltimore Rowhouse by Mary Ellen Hayward and Charles Belfoure

Historic Canton by Norman G. Rukert

Baltimore: The Building of an American City by Sherry H. Olson

Websites

Baltimore City Government
www.ci.baltimore.md.us

Port of Baltimore
www.mpa.state.md.us

Live Baltimore Home Center
www.livebaltimore.com

Butchers Hill Neighborhood Association
www.butchershill.org

Roland Park

Roland Park historical marker

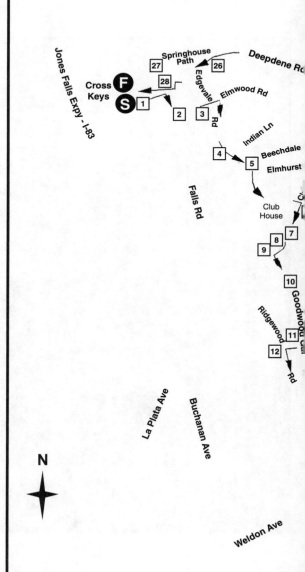

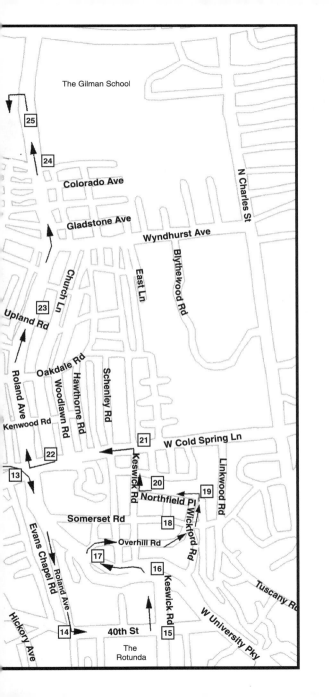

Overview

Distance: Six miles.

Major attractions: The Village of Cross Keys and the community of Roland Park.

Starting location: The guardhouse at the Village of Cross Keys.

Directions to start and parking: From the north, take I-83 (Jones Falls Expressway) south toward downtown Baltimore. Take the Northern Parkway exit. Go east on Northern Parkway. Continue on Northern Parkway for about one-quarter mile. Turn right onto Falls Roads. Continue on Falls Road for about one-half mile. Turn right into the gated main entrance of the Village of Cross Keys and veer right. Parking is located to the right.

From the south, take I-83 north. Take the Cold Spring Lane exit. Go east on Cold Spring Lane. Continue on Cold Spring Lane for about one-quarter mile. Turn left onto Falls Road. Continue on Falls Road for about one mile. Turn left into the main gated entrance of the Village of Cross Keys and veer right. Four-hour visitor parking is available immediately to the right. Additional parking is available past the main gate to the left by Talbots.

Access to eating facilities: Dining facilities are available at the start and finish in the Village of Cross Keys, and along Cold Spring Lane.

Introduction

The Roland Park Hike should only be attempted by those who never tire of seeing fabulously elegant houses in a park-like setting. Roland Park is one of Baltimore's most spectacular neighborhoods. The mere mention of the name conjures images of wealth and prestige. Immaculate homes line most of this hike's six-mile length. What makes Roland Park such an unusual development is that the designers drew inspiration from the beautiful surrounding environment. Homes were built to complement—not detract from—the landscape. Roads trace the land's contours and swerve to avoid towering trees. Natural gardens seamlessly transition from the adjoining woodland. Roland Park is practically devoid of the tightly manicured lawns and sterile ambiance common in more recent suburban developments. A tour through Roland Park is one of Baltimore's premier urban hikes. A word of caution: the Roland Park Hike contains some steep hills (only one substantial incline, however).

1

Begin the hike at the guardhouse in the Village of Cross Keys. Cross over Falls Road. Turn right onto Falls Road Terrace, which is the narrow road paralleling the east side of Falls Road. Continue on Falls Road Terrace for one block.

In the nineteenth century, many taverns and inns hung above their doors a sign bearing a picture of two crossed keys. This was an offering of hospitality that derived from a biblical image of St. Peter's keys. These taverns typically appeared at crossroads and catered to travelers. Crossroad villages containing these taverns came to be called Cross Keys. One such tavern stood at the corner of Falls Road and Cold Spring Lane. It served workers and merchants who took Falls Road in and out of Baltimore City. So when developer James Rouse contemplated a development of houses, offices, and businesses along I-83, he envisioned an inviting village of hospitality, not unlike the former inn located just down Falls Road. This is how the Village of Cross Keys got its name.

The Village of Cross Keys was built in 1962 on what was part of the Baltimore Country Club golf course. It's comprised of hundreds of condominium and townhouse units along with swimming pools, a tennis club, business offices, restaurants, and retail establishments. Popular retail stores in the village include Talbots, Williams-Sonoma, and Heirloom Jewels Ltd. As you exit the village's gated entrance, notice the stone pumphouse to the left, contructed around 1860.

In a June 27, 2000, profile of the Roland Park community, *The Sun* newspaper noted that renowned poet Ogden Nash lived in a townhouse in the Village of Cross Keys from 1965 until his death in 1971. Nash is remembered for coining the phrase "candy is dandy, but liquor is quicker." Nash wrote nineteen books of poetry, many while living in Baltimore. He was also a regular contributor to *The New Yorker* magazine.

2
Turn left onto Elmwood Road.
Continue on Elmwood Road for one block.

Elmwood Road leads into what is officially designated Roland Park. The community is a product of the Roland Park Company, and the brainchild of its general manager, Edward Bouton. Roland Park was built on the former Woodlawn and Oakland estates. The first house was built in 1892, and the community was for the most part completed by 1912. Roland Park was named for Roland Thornberry, a wealthy Englishmen who owned land nearby. He also gave his name to nearby Lake Roland.

Roland Park is sometimes referred to as the country's first suburban development. This is incorrect. In fact, it's not even Baltimore's first suburb. That honor goes to Mt. Washington, which predates Roland Park by forty years. Roland Park, however, can be considered Baltimore's first extensively planned suburban community. It was the first to take a holistic approach to development, accounting for road layout, water, electricity, public transportation, and zoning rules. Roland Park even had an underground sewer system, rare for the day, even though it eventually discharged into Baltimore City's existing open drainage system. And though Roland Park was originally an independent suburban development, it was annexed to the city in 1918.

3

Turn right onto Edgevale Road.
Wind along Edgevale Road for about three blocks.

Notice the unusual variety of houses in Roland Park. Much of Roland Park's allure lies in its eclectic assortment of houses. Georgian mansions perch next to half-timber Tudors, which perch next to Victorians. Unlike tract housing today, the homes in Roland Park were not pre-built. Prospective homeowners purchased the property and then often hired an

---

So Many Rules

The physical condition of many urban neighborhoods ebbs and flows like the tides, but Roland Park has remained constant over time. This can be attributed to the stringent community covenants set forth by Edward Bouton. James F. Waesche, in *Crowning the Gravelly Hill: A History of Roland Park-Guilford-Homeland District*, details the restrictions:

- Houses had to have a forty- to sixty-foot setback.
- Houses along Roland Avenue had to cost at least $5,000 to build; houses on other roads had to cost at least $3,000 (later dropped to $2,600).
- No chicken houses, stables, or outbuildings were allowed.
- Businesses could only be located in the shopping center along Roland Avenue.
- No saloons were allowed anywhere in the neighborhood.
- No cesspools and outhouses were allowed, which were common at the time.
- No private stables were allowed.

Bouton called these his "good sense" covenants, and thought that families abiding by them would make agreeable neighbors. Some Roland Park residents hated the rules and challenged many in courts—unsuccessfully for the most part. But the mint condition of Roland Park today can be attributed in part to Bouton's covenants.

architect to design the house. An architectural committee scrutinized each design to ensure its place in a neighborhood of such caliber. The result is an assortment of dwellings whose one common trait is their impressiveness.

4

In one block, veer left around the traffic island, continuing on Edgevale Road.

5

In one more block, Beechdale Road enters from the left. Continue straight on Edgevale Road.

A two-car stone garage stands at the corner of Edgevale and Beechdale roads. The original covenants of Roland Park disallowed outbuildings of any sort—including garages. Of course, when the covenants were drafted, cars were years away. The automobile eventually gained in popularity, and residents demanded revocation of the covenant outlawing outbuildings. A massive community garage was initially established near the village center, but it proved too inconvenient for those living on the outskirts. Judging by the number of garages scattered about Roland Park, variances to the outbuilding ban were routinely granted. Like the homes here, the garages were designed to be very attractive and as unobtrusive as possible. Even the staircase next to the garage melds nicely into its environs.

Bouton developed Roland Park in six phases. The first one is located east of Roland Avenue. This part of Roland Park was his second phase. To design it Bouton hired the landscape architectural services of Frederick Law Olmsted, Jr., who was the son of the renowned designer of New York City's Central Park. For this section, Olmsted was handed the task of designing a neighborhood around very rugged terrain. His design was a rousing success, and the next few blocks are considered the showcase of Roland Park. Bouton kept Olmsted on to design the remainder of his development. Many of the attributes that endear Baltimoreans to Roland Park were Olmsted's doings.

6

Just past the parking lot for the Baltimore Country Club, Edgevale Road forks to the left. Veer right onto Club Road. Continue on Club Road for one block.

In one block, Upland Road enters from the left. The Roland Park Condominium, formerly one of the community's impressive apartment buildings, stands at the corner of Upland and Club roads. When it was built in 1925, apartment living was considered a desired lifestyle. In *Roland Park: Four Walking Tours and an Informal History*, Priscilla L. Miles notes that one person spent twenty-seven years on the Roland Park Apartments' waiting list before a unit became available. Apartment living eventually lost its luster, and in the 1970s this building was converted into condominium units. Behind the apartment building are the carriage houses that once served as the community stables for Roland Park residents.

The intersection of Upland and Club roads is also where the original water tower serving Roland Park stood. In grand Bouton fashion, the seventy-foot-high tower was topped by an observation deck and wrapped with a decorative iron staircase. Mere functionality without spectacle was unacceptable to Bouton. Water for the neighborhood was drawn from eight artesian wells and several nearby springs, and its quality was considered equal to that of the finest drinking water in the Baltimore area.

7

In front of the clubhouse, continue on Club Road, walking against the one-way direction of Club Road.

Establishment of the Baltimore Country Club, whose clubhouse is to the right, has been called Bouton's masterstroke. Initially, home sales in his development lagged. City denizens had not grasped the appeal of moving to a country house. Bouton had constructed a golf course at this site in 1896, naming it the Roland Park Golf Club. It was designed by Willie Dunn, a professional Scottish golfer. Two years later, Bouton determined the name Roland Park Golf Club was too exclusive, and changed it to the Baltimore Country Club. The name change broadened the golf course's appeal, and Bouton marketed it as a keystone of his development. Golf was experiencing a surge in popularity at the time, and living beside a professionally designed course suddenly proved desirable. Home sales in Roland Park increased. For the family, the club also offered tennis, cricket, bowling, and tobogganing.

The golf course itself is gone. The rugged terrain resulted in too demanding a course, and it was moved down the hill to the flats along Falls Road. The course was then replaced by the Village of Cross Keys and two schools. A wood-shingled clubhouse originally stood along Club Road, but suffered minor fire damage in 1930. During the repair, it burned to the ground. What emerged the same year was the present brick clubhouse, which is among the finest in the Baltimore area.

The half-timber Tudor house directly across from the clubhouse and behind the iron gate, 10 Club Road, was home to the Girls' Latin School from 1927 until its closure in the early 1950s. The counterpart Boys' Latin School of Maryland survives today, and is located north of Roland Park along Lake Avenue.

8

Just past the clubhouse, turn right onto Sunset Path. There is a black sign on the brick wall indicating this pathway. Continue down the stairs on Sunset Path for one block.

Sunset Path is part of a labyrinth of walking paths that snake around Roland Park, revealing hidden gardens and other jewels. This one sneaks behind the estate known as Rusty Rocks. Bouton was given the dilemma of what to do with an unsightly three-acre quarry in the center of his development. Problem solved: he built his own house there. Local fieldstone was Bouton's construction material of choice. His wife did her part, manicuring the grounds into what was considered among the finest show-gardens in the country, which included a pond. Part of the quarry was converted to an amphitheater, where ballets and concerts were held. The quarry's rocky protrusions are visible along Boulder Lane. This unique, understated house stands in stark contrast to the more stately surrounding mansions.

9

Turn left onto Boulder Lane, which is unmarked. Continue on Boulder Lane for one block.

10

At the five-way intersection, continue generally straight ahead onto Goodwood Gardens. Continue on Goodwood Gardens for one block.

Goodwood Gardens stretches for only one block, but it may contain the greatest concentration of impressive dwellings in Baltimore City. A dozen extravagant Georgian mansions, most pillared and stuccoed, line the block, earning its moniker "Millionaire's Row." The entire block was designed by New York architect Charles Platt. The original plan for Goodwood Gardens shows lavish manicured gardens with pathways in each backyard.

11

Turn right onto Kenwood Road. Continue on Kenwood Road for one block.

12

Turn left onto Ridgewood Road. Continue on Ridgewood Road for three blocks.

At 108 Ridgewood Road is the former home of Gideon Stieff, a member of the Baltimore family that manufactured popular silver products. Besides being a wealthy business-man, Stieff also had a knack for farming. Priscilla Miles notes in her book that, as late as World War II, he kept behind his house a menagerie, including chickens, goats, and cows that required daily milking.

Notice the gap between Stieff's house and 104 Ridgewood Road. This was the former site of the Greiner

House—a stunning Georgian mansion. Stieff supposedly had 104 Ridgewood Road built for a relative.

To the left, 103 Ridgewood Road is the beige house with second-story balcony and green shutters. It was Bouton's final residence, where he died in 1941 at the age of 82.

13

Turn right onto Roland Avenue, and immediately cross Cold Spring Lane. Continue on Roland Avenue for about one-half mile. Roland Avenue forks to the right in about one-quarter mile.

The cylindrical structure just past University Parkway is known as the Roland Park Water Tower. The name incorrectly implies that this water tower served the Roland Park community. The tower was completed in 1905 by the city of Baltimore to serve Hampden and adjoining neighborhoods to the south. (Notice that Roland Park is situated uphill of this gravity-feed tank.) Roland Park had its own water tower on Upland Road, near the clubhouse. This water tower along Roland Avenue is no longer in operation, as Baltimore City now employs a reservoir-storage system for its water supply.

14

Turn left onto 40th Street. Continue on 40th Street for one long block.

The quiet residential neighborhood referred to as Wyman Park is to the right. It separates Roland Park from Hampden, and serves as the western boundary of Johns Hopkins University. The residential dwellings of Wyman Park are situated behind The Rotunda, the attractive copper-domed building along 40th Street. The Rotunda building was constructed in 1922 as the headquarters for the Maryland Casualty Company, an insurance agency. The land originally belonged to Johns Hopkins University. When the insurance company outgrew the building in the 1970s, it was converted into a shopping complex featuring a supermarket, about twenty specialty shops, and a cinema that specializes in art-house movies.

To the left is the community referred to as Keswick. The row of three stone buildings hidden on the hill behind the hedgerow belonged to the Roland Park Country School, which was located here from 1916 through 1980. A fire in 1976 that burned the school's main building precipitated the move to its present campus, about one mile north on Roland Avenue. An alley leads from 40th Street just past the third stone building. Sneak up the alley to see the interesting brickwork and architectural details of the third building.

The Keswick Multi-Care Center dominates the northwest intersection of 40th Street and Keswick Road. This institution was incorporated in 1883 as the Home for Incurables of Baltimore City and, according to the sign near its main entrance, was established to "care for and brighten the days of the weary patients of Baltimore city." It was moved to its present location from downtown Baltimore in 1926. At one point it was known as the St. Mary's Female Orphan Asylum. The original buildings are visible, but set back from the road.

15

Turn left onto Keswick Road.
Continue on Keswick Road for one long block.

16

Cross over the southbound lane of University Parkway. Continue for one more block and cross over the northbound lane of University Parkway. Turn left onto University Parkway. Continue on University Parkway for two blocks.

University Parkway was developed by Bouton as the showcase entrance to Roland Park. It was the primary thoroughfare that connected his development with downtown Baltimore, via either Charles Street or St. Paul Street. Bouton made sure that University Parkway was flanked by attractive buildings, including many stately mansions. After you cross over University Parkway, notice the columned yellow Georgian mansion on the hill to the left. It was designed by Charles Platt, who also designed the opulent houses along Goodwood Gardens.

Three colonial mansions line University Parkway to the right. A historic photograph in Waesche's book shows two of these mansions perched on a barren hill amidst a more sparsely developed community. They were built in 1912 at a cost of $23,000 each.

17

Turn right onto Somerset Place and Overhill Road. The road immediately forks. Veer right onto Overhill Road. Continue on Overhill Road for about four blocks.

After veering right, notice the thick and aged vines interwoven into the wrought-iron fence.

18

Turn left onto Wickford Road, walking uphill. Continue on Wickford Road for one block.

19

Turn left onto Northfield Place. Continue on Northfield Place for two blocks, until it dead-ends at Merryman Court.

Like Northfield Place, most of the roads in this part of Roland Park run east-west. This was done by design. Two blocks north of here, across Cold Spring Lane, is the neighborhood referred to as Evergreen. Bouton deemed this community "undesirable." He thought it too low-brow for his more upscale development, and did not want any roads connecting Roland Park with Evergreen. Olmsted's original plan for this part of Roland Park included several north-south thoroughfares extending toward Evergreen. Bouton instructed Olmsted to remove them, which caused a total design overhaul of the neighborhood. In fact, Keswick Road originally extended across University Parkway, but terminated in front of Merryman Court. In 1931, the city extended Keswick Road through to Cold Spring Lane to facilitate quicker fire-response service.

20

Turn right onto Keswick Road. Continue on Keswick Road for two blocks.

21

**Turn left onto Cold Spring Lane.
Continue on Cold Spring Lane for about one-quarter mile.**

Immediately across Cold Spring Lane is the neighborhood of Evergreen, which, contrary to Bouton's opinion, is nothing but charming. Evergreen was the first residential community of this area, predating Roland Park. It was where most laborers who built the Roland Park houses resided. What made the Evergreen neighborhood unusual was that despite its location far from the city's center, and lack of public transportation, it flourished.

Bouton also developed an aversion to Cold Spring Lane, which was an existing road bisecting his development. According to Waesche, he declared that it was an "unimportant street, and we are not proposing to do anything to increase its importance." True to his word, no mansions were placed along this lane. The cluster of busy cafés and coffee shops, however, present an ideal place to take a break. The Video Americain store was the pet shop in the film *The Accidental Tourist*, which was based on a novel of the same title by Anne Tyler, who resides nearby in Homeland.

As you hike along Cold Spring Lane, note the first phase of Bouton's Roland Park development situated to the right. This was the only part of Roland Park developed by Bouton without the designing services of Olmsted. Look down Hawthorne and Woodlawn roads for views of the houses. Unlike Olmsted-designed phases, this part of the community is more conventional in design, and not as conforming to the existing environment. It was designed by George Kessler, a personal friend of Bouton. Houses here are more modest than most others of Roland Park, with most built in the cottage style. This suggests that Bouton's original intent was to develop a quaint upper-middle-class community, and not necessarily the spectacular community into which Roland

Park has evolved. The Roland Springs development to the left was once the site of a large orphanage.

22
Turn right onto Roland Avenue.
Continue on Roland Avenue for about one mile.

Roland Avenue is the wide boulevard bisecting Roland Park. Bouton designed Roland Avenue as a wide, picturesque boulevard partly to accommodate the streetcars that connected his development with downtown Baltimore. As a result, when the automobile arrived, the avenue did not have to be widened, and none of the houses had to be razed. According to Roland Park's original covenants, homes along Roland Avenue had to cost at least $5,000 to build.

The tan house at the northwest intersection of Cold Spring Lane and Roland Avenue, 4500 Roland Avenue, is headquarters of the Roland Park Woman's Club. The club was founded in 1896 by Bouton's wife and friends, but the building wasn't completed until 1903. The social club still functions today.

The dark-colored house at the intersection with Kenwood Road, 4600 Roland Avenue, is one of the few houses in Roland Park that actually predates Bouton's development. This house was part of the original Woodlawn estate on which the neighborhood was built. After a stringent review, the Roland Park Company deemed this house worthy of its community and allowed it to remain.

The white house obscured by trees is 4608 Roland Avenue. It was built by the Roland Park Company in 1900 to serve as a school for the neighborhood children. It later became the Roland Park Country School, which is now located a few blocks north on Roland Avenue.

In Bouton's day, corner lots were always a tough sell. These properties could usually be bought at a discount, which is why so many churches are located on corner lots. Most of Roland Park's churches were built along Roland Avenue. At Oakdale Road is the North Baltimore Mennonite Church on the right, and St. David's Episcopal Church on the left. St.

David's was originally designed to be of the towering Gothic style typical of most turn-of-the-last-century churches. The forward-thinking congregation found those plans unacceptable, and asked for a more progressive design. What resulted was the attractive Renaissance-style sanctuary.

23

Continue on Roland Avenue past Upland Road.

Just past Upland Road is a Tudor-style shopping center. Built in 1894, it's said to be the first shopping center in the United States. Whether this is true depends on how "shopping center" is defined, since many developments built before Roland Park included shopping "arcades." Bouton only allowed businesses necessary for the well-being of his community to operate in the center. Roland Park's covenants restricted shops or restaurants from being situated anywhere else in the neighborhood. The first tenant of the shopping center was Dr. G.W. Truitt, who ran a pharmacy. The pharmacy was later sold and renamed Morgan and Millard's Roland Park Pharmacy, which had an ice-cream bar popular with the neighborhood teens. It's said that many Roland Park residents went on their first date to "The Morg," as it was often referred. The spot later became a popular restaurant that retained the Morgan and Millard's name. Today, it is Petit Louis Bistro. The center also contained a post office, several shops, and a Woman's Exchange, where housewives could sell handicrafts.

This historically significant shopping center almost met its demise in 1975, when its owner attempted to demolish the structure. To expedite his plan, he shut off the heat in hopes of flushing out tenants. Most left immediately. The city intervened in May 1976 by purchasing the building in a condemnation proceeding, and preserved it as a historic landmark.

Visible down Upland Road from the shopping center, with the high yellow-brick pediment, is the original Roland Park fire station. It was built in 1895 and is still in use today. Three holding cells were located behind the fire station, since the closest jailhouse was in Towson, about four miles away.

The intersection of Roland Avenue and Upland Road was the terminus of the trolley that carried Roland Park residents to and from downtown Baltimore. Bouton's ability to get this trolley line extended into Roland Park was partly responsible for the development's success. The trolley turnaround was behind the fire station.

Wyndhurst Avenue to the east side of Roland Avenue serves as Roland Park's northern boundary. Roland Park extends further north on the west side of Roland Avenue, however. The area north of Wyndhurst Road to the east is named Tuxedo Park after a fashionable New York City suburb. The shopping center to the right, which includes the Tuxedo Pharmacy, Eddie's of Roland Park, and Stone Mill Bakery, is a nice spot for a hiking break. Development of Tuxedo Park was in progress two years before ground was broken for Roland Park. It never had the restrictive covenants of Roland Park, though, and the houses there—though certainly beautiful—have a noticeably different appearance.

The Roland Park branch of the Enoch Pratt Free Library stands across from the shopping center. When built in 1921, it was seldom used by residents. Most already had impressive libraries of their own, and many felt that reading circulated books spread germs. It wasn't until the library began purchasing new books that its use increased enough to justify its existence.

24

Roland Avenue intersects Deepdene Road just past the shopping center. Continue on Roland Avenue for one block past Deepdene Road.

Just beyond Deepdene Road begins a stretch of private and public schools. Immediately to the right is the Roland Park Elementary/Middle School, an exceptional member of Baltimore's public school system. Notice the unique green wrought-iron fence along the school's front.

A handful of exclusive private schools huddle along Roland Avenue. Note the sixty-eight-acre Gilman School complex situated just beyond the public school to the right. The Gilman School was originally called the Country School for Boys of Baltimore City, and remains an all-male institution today. The school was founded in 1897 by Anne Galbraith Carey, who thought her son would benefit from a school with a country setting. It was first located on the campus of Johns Hopkins University, but moved to its present location in 1910. At that time, its name was changed to The Gilman Country School for Boys. "Country" was dropped from its title in 1951.

Just about one-half mile behind the Gilman School, twin limestone towers emerge from the foliage. This is the Cathedral of Mary Our Queen. During the great Baltimore fire of 1904, the owner of O'Neill's department store, located on Charles Street in downtown Baltimore, watched helplessly as fire crept toward his establishment. He fled to the Basilica of the Assumption on Cathedral Street and prayed that if his building was spared, he would build a cathedral somewhere in the city. It was, and upon his death he left $8 million for construction of this spectacular church.

Across Roland Avenue from the Gilman School is the Roland Park Country School, an exclusive all-girls academy. This school has a more vagabond history than Gilman. It was established on Keswick Road, moved to Roland Avenue, and onward to University Parkway before settling in its present location in 1980. Though neither the Roland Park Country School nor the Gilman School are technically within the bounds of Roland Park, they are both considered neighborhood fixtures.

Look left into the driveway leading to the Roland Park Country School. The massive limestone building one hill over is St. Mary's Seminary. This institution is one of the oldest in Baltimore City. It was founded in 1791 by priests of the Society of St. Sulpice to educate men entering the Catholic priesthood. Some of the country's most esteemed clergy, including Cardinal Gibbons, graduated from here. The original campus was located in the Seton Hill neighborhood in downtown Baltimore, but it moved here in 1928 and was dedicated a year later. When a new chapel was dedicated in 1964, the event attracted the most important Roman Catholic hierarchy from around the world.

25

**At the traffic light at the entrance to the Roland Park
Country School, backtrack down Roland Avenue for one
block to Deepdene Road. Turn right onto Deepdene Road.
Continue on Deepdene Road for about one-half mile. At that
point, Deepdene Road becomes Edgevale Road. Continue on
Edgevale Road for one block.**

To the right are buildings of the Roland Park Country
School. This was once the estate of Charles J. Bonaparte, the
great nephew of Napoleon. In 1906, when the trolley line
was laid through Roland Park, Bonaparte fled, fearing the
encroachment of the new development. Notice the barn
behind the school buildings; this was an original barn from
Bonaparte's estate.

This road is one of the prettiest in Roland Park. It
provides the best insight into how the development was
finessed into the existing environment. Each home seems to
embrace the surrounding hillside. Near the bottom of the
hill, notice the great number of steps required to get from the
road to the front door of some homes.

26

**Turn right onto Springhouse Path. Continue on Springhouse
Path for one block, until it dead-ends at Falls Road.**

27

**Turn left onto Falls Road.
Continue on Falls Road for about 100 feet.**

28

**Turn right into the main gated entrance to the
Village of Cross Keys. This hike ends at the guardhouse
to the Village of Cross Keys.**

Suggested Reading

Books

Crowning the Gravelly Hill: A History of the Roland Park-Guilford-Homeland District by James F. Waesche

Roland Park: Four Walking Tours and an Informal History by Priscilla L. Miles

Reflections on Roland Park by Community Research and Development

Jones Falls in Mt. Washington

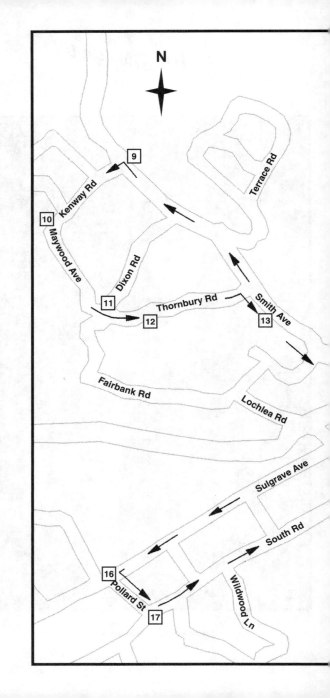

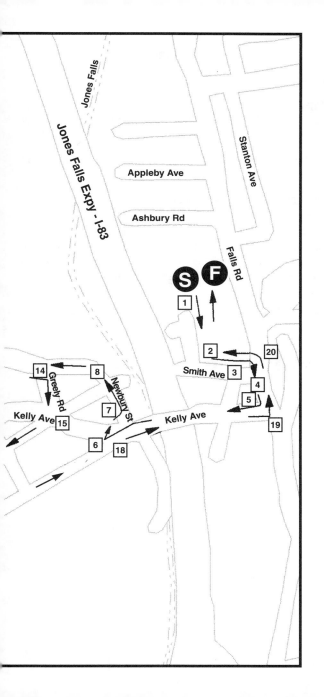

Overview

Distance: Three miles.

Major attractions: Mt. Washington Mill shopping complex; Mt. Washington Village; and the adjoining neighborhoods that once served as a summer retreat for Baltimore City's wealthy.

Starting location: The parking lot of the Mt. Washington Mill complex.

Directions to start and parking: From Baltimore City, take I-83 north. Take the Northern Parkway exit east. Continue on Northern Parkway for one block. Turn left onto Falls Road. Continue on Falls Road for one-half mile. Turn left onto Smith Avenue, which is one block past Kelly Avenue. Continue on Smith Avenue past the mill complex. Smith Avenue dead-ends in a parking lot, which is where this hike begins.

From the north, take I-83 south toward downtown Baltimore. Take the Northern Parkway exit east, and follow the directions above.

Access to eating facilities: The Mt. Washington Mill complex, where the hike begins and ends, has a Starbucks Coffee and Whole Foods Market. Several restaurants can be found in Mt. Washington Village.

Introduction

Mt. Washington was Baltimore's first true suburban development. It was conceived in 1854 by real estate developer George Gelbach, who predicted that the high and unspoiled hills to the north of downtown Baltimore would attract city dwellers seeking respite from the oppressive urban summers. Gelbach called his resort the Mt. Washington Rural Retreat. Marketing literature, titled "Description of Mount Washington Rural Retreat on the Baltimore and Susquehanna Railroad and Falls Turnpike," touted the gently rolling hills as abounding in "many springs of the purest waters, and several handsomely winding streams," which would be "tastefully ornamented into artificial lakes, water-falls, fountains, etc." According to Gelbach, the "grounds are laid off with fine, broad Avenues, Promenades, Carriage-drives, Lakes, Water-falls, Fountains," and railroad trains were "constantly going back and forth" between here and the city.

Gelbach may have padded the truth with regard to the retreat's offerings, but his foresight was undeniable. Well-heeled city denizens by the dozens fled to Gelbach's retreat, building lavish mansions tucked in the shaded hillsides. H.L. Mencken was among the notable seasonal immigrants. Summer residents quickly became year-round dwellers thanks to the proximity of the passenger train to downtown Baltimore. Today many Baltimoreans think of Mt. Washington as little more than some specialty shops and cafés in the village, and a Starbucks Coffee and Whole Foods Market across the railroad tracks. The true Mt. Washington, however, also includes the dozens of spectacular nineteenth-century mansions, which remain hidden in the hillsides surrounding the village. This hike will reveal the essence of Mt. Washington as envisioned by George Gelbach.

1

The hike begins in the parking lot of the Mt. Washington Mill complex. Walk toward Whole Foods Market and Starbucks Coffee.

When the affluent arrived in Mt. Washington starting in 1854, a vibrant blue-collar mill town already existed on the banks of Jones Falls. The area around the mill complex was once the town of Washingtonville. Imagine an array of residences and businesses fanning out across the Jones Falls floodplain along a grid of streets. Washingtonville was established to serve the large mill whose buildings line the south of the parking lot (now occupied by Starbucks Coffee, Whole Foods Market, and other businesses). For a century Washingtonville not only survived, but flourished. A slow bleed began in the 1920s, however, when the mill ceased operations. Washingtonville met its ultimate demise in the late 1950s at the hands of urban planners, who chose to slice the I-83 expressway right through its heart. The town was for the most part dismantled and relegated to the status of ghost town.

The only residential dwelling of Washingtonville to escape eradication is the brick duplex to the north of the mill buildings, now occupied by a picture framing shop. This house stands on Forge Avenue, which was once the main street of Washingtonville. As evidenced by historical photographs, most houses in the former town were Federal-style two-story duplexes and rowhouses, similar to those still found in Baltimore's other working-class neighborhoods, such as Canton, Highlandtown, and South Baltimore.

The mill that provided Washingtonville its livelihood belonged to the Washington Cotton Manufacturing Company. It was one of the largest of the dozens of mills that lined Jones Falls into downtown Baltimore. The Washington Cotton Manufacturing Company started its 288 spindles spinning in 1810 as Maryland's first cotton mill, and the first in the nation to be powered by water. Starbucks Coffee occupies the former boiler building, where coal was converted to steam. Next door is the engine building, where the steam was

The Love of Mt. Washington

The game of lacrosse may have been invented by Native Americans, but it would be tough to argue with anyone sitting on a Mt. Washington Tavern barstool that this tiny village isn't the center for the sport. For about a century, lacrosse has been Mt. Washington's greatest source of pride. The Mt. Washington Lacrosse Club played its first game in 1904, and within a few years was considered the finest team in the nation. Their perennial rival was Long Island's Crescent Athletic Club, composed of Canadian hotshots. The Mt. Washington club's original field was situated along the railroad tracks to the south of town, on the grounds of the former Baltimore Cricket Club. The field, along with the club's fanciful wood-shingled clubhouse, was lost to the construction of I-83. The replacement field and brick clubhouse are visible from I-83, just north of the Northern Parkway exit. The Wolfpack, as the Mt. Washington club is known, remains the oldest post-collegiate lacrosse club in the world, and the most successful. It has won a dozen United States Club Lacrosse Association championships since the league's inception in 1960. Club members regularly represent the national team in the world championships.

harnessed into kinetic energy. The existing cupola on the mill's main stone building contained a bell that each morning tolled the townsfolk to their work stations. Prior to the Civil War, the Washington Cotton Manufacturing Company produced cotton duck, which was the thick canvas-like material used in ship sails. Some of the final products were sold in a shop on South Charles Street, near Baltimore's waterfront. After the war, the mill was bought by a conglomeration that was producing almost 80 percent of the country's cotton duck. The former millrace originally extended across what is now the parking lot, and Jones Falls over time has been reduced to a trickle of its former self due to distressed water usage.

2
Cut in between Whole Foods Market
and Starbucks Coffee.

The metal sculpture on the far side of the mill buildings was crafted by Rory McCarthy of Sonoma, California, using nuts, bolts, and other hardware left over from the Maryland Bolt and Nut Company, which took over some mill buildings in the 1920s when mill operations ceased. McCarthy was in town designing the Smith and Hawken building, which is behind the sculpture. The low brick building facing Smith Avenue housed offices for the Maryland Bolt and Nut Company. Notice the inscription across its main entrance.

3
Turn left onto Smith Avenue.
Continue on Smith Avenue for one block.

Across Smith Avenue is the stone and wood-frame Mt. Washington United Methodist Church, which has survived life on the Jones Falls floodplain since its construction in 1860. The congregation was actually established in 1852, but worshiped elsewhere until this sanctuary was built. Behind the church is Mt. Washington's recreational complex, which includes the Meadowbrook Aquatic and Fitness Center, and the Northwest Family Sports Center, which contains an ice rink. The Meadowbrook Club was the training facility for Anita Nall, who won three medals in the 1992 summer Olympics in Barcelona, Spain. Beyond the swim club is Norris Field, home to the Mt. Washington Lacrosse Club.

Western Run flows into Jones Falls along Smith Avenue. Western Run is the smaller tributary, and originates in the hills west of Mt. Washington Village. Jones Falls has its source near Owings Mills, but traces an arc across Baltimore County before swinging due south through Baltimore City. It's the most significant tributary to Baltimore's Inner Harbor, entering just east of the Hard Rock Café. The flow of Jones Falls is blocked about a mile upstream of Mt. Washington by the Lake Roland dam in Robert E. Lee Park.

4

Turn right onto Falls Road.
Continue on Falls Road for one block.

5

Turn right onto Kelly Avenue. Continue on Kelly Avenue for
one long block, across the Kelly Avenue Bridge.

The Kelly Avenue Bridge connects Falls Road with Mt. Washington Village. It was built in 1926 as a means to move both streetcars and automobiles across Jones Falls and the Northern Central Railroad tracks. The 800-foot-long bridge was widened in 1977. The Kelly Avenue Bridge also passes over I-83 (Jones Falls Expressway), which connects the Baltimore beltway north of the city with the downtown business district. Built in the late 1950s, I-83 relieved automobile congestion north of the city. It also relieved scores of Mt. Washington and Washingtonville residents of their homes and businesses. Kelly Avenue is thought to be named for Simon Kelly, a signal operator for the railroad company in the late nineteenth century, who was given the responsibility of assuring safe traffic flow around nearby railroad crossings.

When the Mt. Washington Rural Retreat was developed in the mid-1800s, no bridge crossed Jones Falls. To move from the mill town to the shops along Falls Road (which was Baltimore's primary north/south artery) required fording Jones Falls, which townsfolk did regularly. The first bridge to cross Jones Falls in the Mt. Washington area was built in 1884. It was an iron truss bridge erected to connect Charles Street with Reisterstown Road—two of Baltimore's busiest thoroughfares at the time. It was built on Belvedere Road, which once crossed Jones Falls just downstream of Mt. Washington.

6

Just past the Kelly Avenue Bridge, take a sharp right into Mt. Washington Village on the Kelly Avenue extension. Continue on the Kelly Avenue extension for one block.

Just beyond the Kelly Avenue Bridge is the St. John's Episcopal Church, which opened its doors in 1869. Construction of the bridge displaced the original wooden church building, along with several other businesses and houses. Parishioners rejoiced, however, as their new building was larger and more solidly built. The exit off the bridge marks the beginning of Mt. Washington Village, which is the town's main business area. The enclave is home to numerous cafés, offices, and specialty shops.

Mt. Washington Village is thriving now, but fell into disrepair over the middle part of the twentieth century. It experienced a renaissance in the 1970s. Walkways were paved and streetcar tracks were removed. Bright streetlights were installed, and shops were given new facades. Mt. Washington Village became once again a desirable destination—not only for its own residents, but for those from nearby Ruxton and Roland Park as well.

7

Turn left onto Newbury Street. Continue on Newbury Street for two blocks.

McCafferty's Pub is located to the right in the gray Catalyst Square building. Notice the vintage autographed footballs and helmets displayed in the windows, including those of Bart Starr, Gale Sayers, Y.A. Tittle, and local icon Johnny Unitas. The pub is named for former Baltimore Colt's coach Don McCafferty and is owned by his son. It remains a hangout for fans of the Baltimore Ravens professional football team. Local sports radio talk shows occasionally broadcast from McCafferty's Pub.

Cross Sulgrave Avenue, and look left for an interesting assortment of brightly hued shops and cafés, including Crepe du Jour, The Desert Café, and Ethel and Ramone's. Just past

Sulgrave Avenue is the Mt. Washington Tavern. Until the village's renaissance, Mt. Washington Tavern was a blue-collar watering hole, complete with pool tables and a dingy linoleum floor. During the 1970s revitalization, it received a makeover, and became a trendy pub, popular with the local lacrosse crowd. It remains one of the best places to grab a bite in the village.

The stone building to the right, peeking out from behind the Europa International Salon, is Mt. Washington's former fire station. Mt. Washington was annexed to Baltimore City in 1919, but the need to establish a firehouse was established before then. In 1891, a major hotel and store in the village burned down. Urgent consideration was given to establishing a firehouse in town. Land for the station was donated from a nearby estate. Ironically, before construction of the firehouse commenced, Glen Mary, the spacious mansion of the estate, burned to the ground. The firehouse was ostensibly built in the stone building behind the Europa International Salon. It also contained the courthouse and three holding cells. Today, the building is used as office space.

The Mt. Washington Station of the light rail is at the intersection of Newbury Street and Smith Avenue. The light rail runs from Hunt Valley clear through Baltimore City to the Baltimore Washington International Airport. Rail service had been a mainstay of life for Mt. Washington residents for almost a century. The area's proximity to the Northern Central Railroad line (formerly called the Baltimore and Susquehanna Railroad line), which connected downtown Baltimore with York, Pennsylvania, allowed summer visitors to assume permanent residency here. That line ceased operations in 1956. It took four decades to renew interest in a passenger line serving Mt. Washington, this one in the form of the light rail.

8

Turn left onto Smith Avenue.
Continue on Smith Avenue for one-half mile.

Smith Avenue was laid out in the 1830s as a means to connect Falls Road with Reisterstown Road to the west. The former Mt. Washington branch of the Enoch Pratt Free Library stands at the corner of Smith Avenue and Greely Road, in an ornate stone and brick building. This library served Mt. Washington residents starting in 1921. Around 1950, with overcrowding of public schools a problem in the village, Baltimore City proposed to annex the library as a classroom. A heated battle ensued, with angry words tossed about in the editorial sections of Baltimore's newspapers. "Hell hath no fury like a Mt. Washingtonian battling for his library," wrote one reporter. Library patrons argued that the institution was partially set up with funds donated by philanthropist Andrew Carnegie, who demanded that library service be provided at that location. The Board of Trustees of the Enoch Pratt Free Library argued that the books were old and not very "technical" in nature. After several court battles, the city emerged victorious, placing a classroom there in 1951. The village was compensated with a bookmobile that roamed its streets. Today, the library building is home to Baltimore Clayworks, a nationally renowned non-profit organization promoting the artistic creation of pottery. Exhibits are available for inspection in the building across Smith Avenue.

The Shrine of the Sacred Heart Church stands at 5800 Smith Avenue, just past Greely Road. This Tudor-Gothic structure replicates an English country chapel where the poet Thomas Gray once wrote "Elegy Written in a Country Churchyard." The church began in 1855 in a wooden building across Smith Avenue. It remains a vital community institution today, and includes a private primer school. The unique house with a steep-pitched roof at 1701 Regent Road, set back from Smith Avenue and just past the church, serves as its rectory. This area was where Glen Mary stood, the spacious mansion destroyed in the turn-of-the-last-century blaze.

An entrance to Mt. Washington Conference Center is across Smith Avenue from the church. About one hundred yards past this entrance, look high on the hill to the right. The oddly shaped four-story brick building, encircled with layers of verandas, is the Octagonal House, built in 1856 on Mt. Washington's highest point. It originally housed the Mt. Washington Female College, which was established to "finish" the education of southern belles, offering subjects considered civil and gracious. The college could not survive the Civil War, and stood vacant for some time. It was purchased in 1867 by the Sisters of Mercy for use as the Mt. St. Agnes College. The original octagonal building became a mere adjunct, as many other buildings were constructed to serve as classrooms and dormitories. In 1972, the complex was purchased by the United States Fidelity and Guaranty Corporation (now the St. Paul Companies) for use as a conference center. The Octagonal House was designed by Thomas Dixon, who also designed the gothic Mt. Vernon Methodist Church on Mt. Vernon Square in downtown Baltimore.

Ascend Smith Avenue. Orson Squire Fowler's influence on local architecture can be seen in several of the duplex dwellings to the left, including 5920/22 Smith Avenue and 5924/26 Smith Avenue. Although these are not truly octagonal houses, each possesses obvious octagonal characteristics.

Pass Thornbury Road, and look left up the hill. This is the Dixon Hill development, one of the first in Mt. Washington. The hill was developed by brothers Thomas and James Dixon beginning in 1855, soon after they bought the deed to the mountain from Gelbach. Houses on Dixon Hill are among the finest in Mt. Washington, not only because of their size and design, but also because of how discreetly they perch among the hill's natural features. Since the houses' primary function was to elude the summer swelter, they tend to be airy and shaded, with large windows for ventilation. Many residents sought land on the higher elevations of the hill, arguing that the air there was cooler and healthier. This hike will return down Thornbury Road after passing through the Dixon Hill development. Details of various mansions hidden in the hills around Mt. Washington can be found in

Mt. Washington's Octagonal Buildings

Orson Squire Fowler was a leading nineteenth-century phrenologist. Phrenology is the interpretation of human nature through studying the shape of an individual's skull. Phrenologists believe that a person's mental faculties are tied to head shape, and some say they may loosely be considered the equivalent of today's psychiatrists. Fowler's lasting impression on society, however, came not from his fetish for head-shape, but through his avocation, which was architecture. In 1848, Fowler published *A Home For All*, which espoused the virtues of the octagonal house. Fowler argued through mathematical equations and reason that eight-sided houses not only optimized space, but heat, light, and ventilation as well. His persuasiveness began a trend, as thousands of octagonal houses, churches, and schools were built across the nation, several in the Mt. Washington area. The unique and beautiful Octagonal House on the campus of the Mt. Washington Conference Center, and several Mt. Washington residences, owe their existence to Fowler's vision and ingenuity. The octagonal fad was short-lived, however. A recession in 1857 halted house construction, and Fowler's book—and with it, his idea—eventually went out of print.

Mark Miller's book, *Mt. Washington: Baltimore Suburb*, from which much of the following information was drawn.

9

Turn left onto Kenway Road. Continue on Kenway Road for one block up the steep incline.

10

At the top of the hill, Kenway Road veers left and becomes Maywood Avenue. Continue on Maywood Avenue for one block.

11

After one block, Maywood Avenue becomes Thornbury Road. Continue on Thornbury Road for one block. Do not turn left down Dixon Road.

12

After one block, Thornbury Road takes a sharp left down a steep decline. Continue downhill on Thornbury Road. Before that, swing right through the parking area.

The first houses built on Dixon Hill were 1813 and 1815 Thornbury Road. They were erected in 1855, shortly after the Dixons purchased the deed to the hill from George Gelbach. A recession caused by the threat of civil war suppressed the housing market, and sales on Dixon Hill lagged. Construction on the hill was halted for almost a decade. In 1873, construction of houses began again, possibly because the Dixons held interest in a lumber company and wanted to put its lumber to use. By the 1880s, sixteen houses and a church dotted Dixon Hill. The hill just southwest of Dixon Hill, along Kelly Avenue, also harbored beautiful mansions. This development was referred to as Pill Hill for the many doctors who settled there.

The herringbone-shingled building with slate-gray roof near the bottom of Thornbury Road was formerly Mt. Washington Presbyterian Church. It was built in 1878 by John Dixon, shortly after the partial dissolution of St. John's Episcopal Church in the village. Since the late 1960s, it has housed The Chimes, an agency that provides residential space, vocational training, and other services to special-needs individuals. As you descend Thornbury Avenue near The Chimes, note the fine views of the Octagonal House across Smith Avenue.

13

**Turn right onto Smith Avenue.
Continue on Smith Avenue for two blocks.**

14

**Turn right onto Greely Road.
Continue on Greely Road for one block.**

Greely Road crosses Western Run, a tributary to Jones Falls. About one-half mile upstream from this crossing, near what is now Cross Country Boulevard, was Mt. Washington's other important mill. This one produced tobacco, and was started in 1855 by Manuel Thomas Forsyth, an experienced cigar-maker, and his partner Louis Cole. For more than a decade, the partners sold tobacco products bearing the label "Virginia Tobacco." A calamitous flood demolished the mill in 1868, and it was not rebuilt.

15

Turn right onto Sulgrave Avenue. Continue on Sulgrave Avenue for about four blocks.

Sulgrave Avenue, formerly called North Avenue, leads through yet another pocket of fantastic Mt. Washington mansions. To the far west end of Sulgrave Avenue is Mt. Washington Heights, an attractive residential community built in the 1920s.

The new house to the left, 1709 Sulgrave Avenue, has replaced one of Mt. Washington's most spectacular Victorian mansions, built in the mid-1870s by musician Henry Schwing. Detailed like a gingerbread house and loaded with Gothic features, including impressive gables, it was considered Mt. Washington's finest example of Gothic-Victorian architecture. Like several other wood-constructed Mt. Washington mansions, it failed to endure the test of time and was razed.

Directly across from Mt. Washington Elementary School, 1808 Sulgrave Avenue is a dark-shingled octagonal house hidden behind a hedgerow. Like the Octagonal House at the conference center, this dwelling owes its existence to the vision of Orson Fowler. William Yardley, for whom the house was built, was a railroad engineer with the Northern Central Railroad. It's said that all three of Yardley's daughters fought ferociously for the front bedroom in the new house. Yardley turned to Fowler's plan to solve this dilemma; he built an octagonal house, where every room was a front room. His daughters were satisfied, and Yardley was rewarded with one of Mt. Washington's most distinctive houses.

16
Turn left onto Pollard Street, near a brown and white garage. Continue on Pollard Street for one block.

17
**Turn left onto South Road.
Continue on South Road for about four blocks.**

Before turning left onto South Road, look right for one of Mt. Washington's most impressive houses. The brown-pillared 2100 South Road was built by General Thomas Shyrock in 1895. Shyrock earned his stripes in the National Guard and amassed his wealth through a lumber business. He was also Maryland's first elected Republican state treasurer. An original house on this site was destroyed by a ferocious storm, and a subsequent version quickly succumbed to fire. Shyrock, obviously not a superstitious man, deemed the site perfect for construction of a grand mansion worthy of his wealth and stature. For an interesting vantage, walk up South Road to the front entrance.

After a left turn onto South Road, the second right is Roxbury Place, which is a discreet lane that can be easily missed. Roxbury Place disappears into dense woods, but presents an interesting diversion; about 100 yards down is an unusual pair of Swiss chalet-style cottages.

Just past where Roxbury Place enters from the right stands 1912 South Road. The house was once referred to as "The Cedars," and was a popular summer boarding house for city dwellers. It is thought that the original building on this site was razed and replaced by the present structure, possibly in the late 1860s. Although the original house was built in 1854, architectural features of the present dwelling—the turret and window frame types, for example—are reminiscent of the later period.

Developer John Graham built many of the houses along Sulgrave Avenue and South Road. He arrived at Mt. Washington soon after the Civil War on his doctor's orders. Graham suffered through years of bronchial illness, and his doctor thought the pure air and high elevation of Mt.

Washington would help clear his lung ailments. He built 1813 South Road as his primary residence, which later became known as "The New Oaks." Graham opened his house to summer and autumn boarders, and it soon became a social center of Mt. Washington. Esteemed Baltimore artist Charles Yardley frequented the dwelling, and invited other local artists for sketching parties. The New Oaks has since been carved into apartments, but the windowpane above the front entrance still indicates its nickname.

To the left is 1812 South Road, just past where Helendale Street enters. It was built in 1877, and later served as the residence of Theodore Marburg, who was the United States' ambassador to Belgium.

Home of the former Rugby School, 1806 South Road was one of Mt. Washington's first institutions of learning. Classes began in 1854 under the tutelege of Edwin Arnold, a Washington, D.C., school teacher, who thought its rural setting provided the ideal location to achieve an education. This private school catered to Arnold's idea of what comprised the perfect education—philosophy, geography, history, bookkeeping, arithmetic, and several languages including Greek and Latin. The school lasted only a few years, mostly due to the disruptive threat of civil war.

Lochlea Road enters South Road from the left. Just beyond this intersection, at 1705 South Road, is the stunning estate that was home to Mt. Washington Rural Retreat's founder, George Gelbach. The original residence included a large Italianate cupola and a personal four-story water tower, fed by a stream crossing the backyard. Gelbach lived here only a short time before returning to another residence in Baltimore City. Since then, this estate has housed a long series of prominent owners, and was site of some key events. In 1870, the bishops of the Episcopal Diocese of Maryland declared that vestrymen of all their churches must be of the Episcopal denomination. Those expelled from nearby St. John's Episcopal Church met here, and formed the Mt. Washington Presbyterian Church (which now houses The Chimes).

18

South Road merges onto Kelly Avenue, just before the bridge. Continue on Kelly Avenue over the bridge.

19

**Turn left onto Falls Road.
Continue on Falls Road for one block.**

20

Turn left onto Smith Avenue. Continue on Smith Avenue, past the mill complex, until it dead-ends in a parking lot. The hike ends in the parking lot of the Mt. Washington Mill complex.

Suggested Reading

Books

Mt. Washington: Baltimore Suburb by Mark Miller

The Story of Mt. Washington, Maryland by B. Latrobe Weston

Towson

Towson intersection

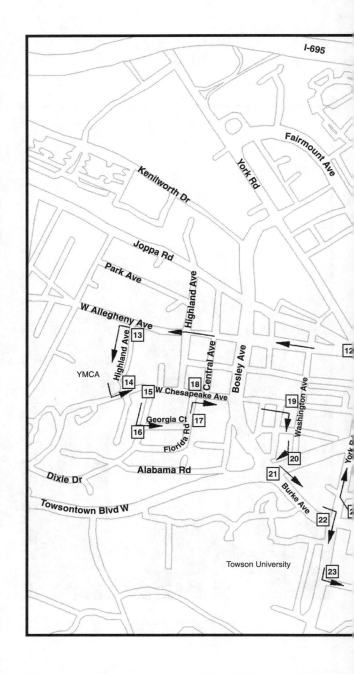

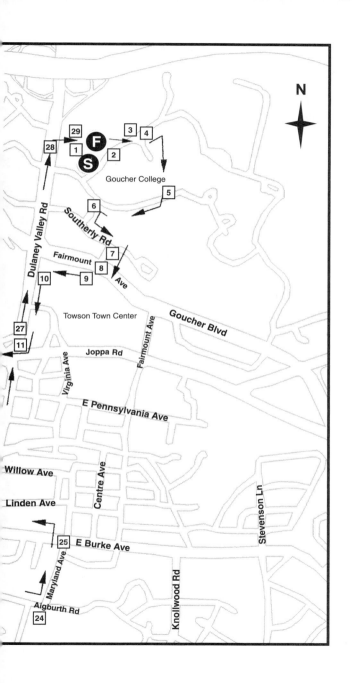

Overview

Distance: Five-and-one-half miles.

Major attractions: Goucher College; the Towson Town Center shopping mall; historic downtown Towson; and Towson University.

Starting location: The visitors' parking lot at Goucher College.

Directions to start and parking: Take the I-695 beltway to the north of Baltimore. Take Exit 27, Dulaney Valley Road, south, heading inside the beltway. Continue south on Dulaney Valley Road for about one-quarter mile. Turn left into the main entrance of Goucher College. Just past the security gate, turn left into the visitors' parking lot, which is clearly marked.

Access to eating facilities: A variety of interesting eateries are located throughout Towson. Most are located along York Road and Allegheny Avenue.

Introduction

The story of Towson begins like that of so many other Maryland towns. A farming community forms around a crossroad; a warren of inns and businesses emerges to suit the needs of travelers; and a quaint village blossoms, which eventually evolves into a more substantial town. See Catonsville, Ellicott City, Frederick, and Bel Air for examples of this progression.

But the story of Towson does not end there. It continues on to the next page, to the part about accelerating growth and urbanization. Towering skyscrapers and sprawling shopping centers went up across town. Streets were widened and major institutions established. Today, from the beltway, Towson appears to be a monolith of steel and glass, about to sink under its own weight. But this unique evolution has provided Towson with a distinct niche: it's an urban environment in the suburbs. Its busy streets harbor energy and bustle on a level found in downtown Baltimore, yet its surrounding residential neighborhoods remain quiet and placid. Few other places combine the effervescence of an urban environment with the intimacy of a suburban setting. This unique combination makes Towson a fascinating place to poke around in.

1

Begin the hike in the visitors' parking lot of Goucher College.

2

Facing the stone buildings of Goucher College, walk to the left end of the parking lot. Cross over the grass border, and turn right onto the loop road that circles campus. Continue on the loop road toward the stone classroom buildings.

Goucher College was once considered to be among the nation's elite women's colleges. That all changed in 1986, however, when the descision was made to admit male students, to the reluctance of many students and alumni (the first was admitted in the Spring of 1987). Despite the change, Goucher College still retains its stature as a premier co-educational liberal arts school.

Goucher College was founded in 1885 as the Woman's College of Baltimore City. Its original campus was on 23rd Street in downtown Baltimore, around Charles and St. Paul streets. Some of the original buildings are now occupied by the Maryland Geological Survey. Women's colleges were unusual at that time. Many thought a collegiate education was too demanding for women; some considered higher education for women too liberal. Mary Cecilia Fisher and her husband, the Reverend Dr. John Franklin Goucher, thought otherwise. Fisher was a wildly wealthy Cecil County denizen, and her husband had a philanthropic heart. Together, they funded numerous Maryland charitable and civic programs. They donated about $700,000 to help establish and maintain the Woman's College of Baltimore City—a substantial sum for the late 1800s. Goucher College remained in Baltimore City until 1954, when the entire operation moved to Towson. Each building on the Goucher College campus is identified by a blue sign on its front lawn.

3

Continue on the loop road past the Hoffberger Science Center.

Just past the Hoffberger Science Center is the Julia Rodgers Library. One of Towson's grandest mansions once stood here. The Epsom mansion was a three-story showplace with a facade that featured two glass-walled conservancies flanking a columned portico. It was built in the early nineteenth century, but succumbed a century later to fire. A cannon of the type used in the Revolutionary War, removed from a local disbanded armory in 1830, stood on the front lawn of Epsom. After the fire, the cannon evidently sank into the earth. It was uncovered in 1951 during excavation of the Julia Rodgers Library. The cannon once graced the front lawn of the library, but the whereabouts today could not be ascertained.

4

**Just past the Chapel, turn right onto the walking path.
Continue on the walking path to the
front entrance of the Chapel.**

As you pass alongside the Chapel, observe that buildings to the left are generally dormitories and student services, and those to the right, classrooms. Notice the interesting stonework in the pediment above the Chapel's entrance. If the doors are open, pop in for a peek at the interior.

5

**Continue on the walking path away from the Chapel.
About fifty feet past the gazebo, turn left onto another
walking path. Continue on this walking path for
about one hundred feet, until it dead-ends at
the loop road. Turn right onto the loop road.**

The campus of Goucher College is bordered by a thick ribbon of woodland. The original 1951 campus was 421 acres. Some of this acreage has been sold off to build adjoining shopping centers. Nonetheless, Goucher still maintains about 300 acres of grounds, many of the them wooded and laced with trails. It's not uncommon to have horses, mountain bikes, and deer competing for the trails.

6

**Continue on the loop road, exiting campus through the
security gate. Just past the security gate, turn left onto an
unnamed road. Continue on this road for one block until it
dead-ends in front of a parking garage. Turn left onto
Southerly Road, which is also unmarked. Continue on
Southerly Road for one block, following signs for Towson.**

7

Turn right onto Towson Gate Drive. Continue on Towson Gate Drive for one block, until it dead-ends at Fairmount Avenue.

8

Continue across Fairmount Avenue, through the parking lot of the Towson Town Center shopping mall. Enter the mall through the high arched entrance to your left.
(Note: to bypass the mall, turn right onto Fairmount Avenue and left onto Dulaney Valley Road. Continue past the Mobil gas station on Dulaney Valley Road.)

A trip to Towson is not complete without a romp through one of its shopping facilities. The four-level Towson Town Center may be the most popular shopping mall in the Baltimore area. It features two anchor department stores—Hecht's and Nordstrom—and over 200 other specialty shops and restaurants. The mall includes over 4,000 parking spaces. It was originally built in 1959, but has undergone several major expansions. The most recent was in 1991, when the third and fourth levels were added. Towson Town Center is a product of The Rouse Company, which also brought to Maryland the Harborplace waterfront development in Baltimore and much of the city of Columbia.

9

Continue to the main mall corridor. Turn right onto the main corridor. In about fifty yards, take the escalators to the second floor. After exiting the escalator, turn right. Continue toward the Rainforest Café sign. Exit the mall through the doors near the Rainforest Café's entrance.

10

In the mall's parking lot, veer left and then turn right around the parking garage. Cross the parking lot to Dulaney Valley Road. Turn left onto Dulaney Valley Road, walking uphill toward Towson Circle.

11

Just past Hecht's department store and the Towson Town Center parking garage, turn right onto Towson Circle. Follow the circle counter-clockwise. Cross over York and Joppa roads.

Towson Circle is historically one of the busiest intersections in Baltimore County. It is where York, Joppa, and Dulaney Valley roads intertwine. Joppa Road is a former Indian trail that slices across the county. Towson Circle was home to Towson's first business—the three-story, thirteen-room Towson Hotel built in 1768 by Ezekiel Towson. Later, owners of the hotel successfully petitioned that the York Turnpike (now York Road) run past the front door of the inn by donating land for the turnpike construction. Deep pockets carried political sway even in the eighteenth century. As a result, the Towson Hotel and tavern thrived until it was demolished in 1929. In their book *Towson and the Village of Ruxton and Lutherville*, Molly O'Donovan and Brooke Gunning note farmers moving livestock from the northern county farms to Baltimore City were frequent clients of the Towson Hotel. According to the authors, many cattle spent their final evening there.

Cross York Road and look right. The stone building on the left side of the road is Towson's oldest standing structure, dating to about 1790. The Schmuck House once served as the original toll house for the York Turnpike. Members of the namesake Towson family later occupied the house.

12

Turn right onto Allegheny Avenue. Continue on Allegheny Avenue for about six blocks.

Allegheny Avenue is lined with an interesting assortment of cafés and specialty shops. At the end stands the twenty-seven-story Penthouse high-rise, at 28 Allegheny Avenue. The Penthouse is indicative of the glass and steel construction that swept Towson in the 1970s. The Penthouse was considered a utopian community of condominiums, offices, parking, and retail space. Many other such skyscrapers were built around Towson. Some say they collectively suffocate the historical quaintness of the village.

Much of the urban renewal effort was spearheaded by Towson's most well-known citizen, Spiro Agnew. Agnew served as Vice President under Richard Nixon, but began his political career as Baltimore County Executive, and, later, Governor of Maryland. Agnew was gracious to his hometown, funding tens of millions of dollars worth of renewal projects. What made Towson ripe for renewal was its position as county seat, combined with its assortment of anchor foundations, such as two colleges and three hospitals.

Just past Washington Avenue is Trinity Episcopal Church. This is the oldest church building still standing in Towson. It was built in 1860 of local limestone. Most local churches built in the late nineteenth century reflected a strong revival of Gothic architecture, which replicates the style used for medieval structures. Notice the narrow windows of the church towers. These resemble the slit windows found in medieval castles through which bows could easily discharge arrows. In the early 1900s, Trinity Episcopal Church was enlarged to a cruciform shape by adding two transepts and extending the nave. Next door to the church is the Surprise Shop, which is a thrift store operated by the church. The Victorian building was the original church rectory, built in 1883.

Notice the unusual private residence at 506 Baltimore Avenue, with the concave mansard roof and the circular windows. As you pass the house, look at the Victorian gazebo top peeking over the high privacy wall.

Bosley Avenue is part of a micro beltway that was intended to completely circle Towson's downtown historic and business district, ridding the downtown district of traffic. Inspection of a Towson map reveals that one segment of the beltway was never completed—the stretch through east Towson, which is Towson's African-American community. The neighborhoods there successfully stopped the beltway from slicing through their community, which would have caused the mass displacement of citizens at a time when minorities were often the victims of such civil works projects. The widening of Bosley Avenue and other major arteries through Towson caused the razing of a tremendous number of spectacular mansions. Many mansions that did survive the renewal have been converted to office space.

The unusual stone building just past Bosley Avenue belongs to the Woman's Club of Towson, which is a non-political, non-sectarian social and civic organization. The building was constructed in 1909 as a Methodist Church. The Woman's Club took over the building in 1934, soon after the club's formation. The club was responsible for, among other things, establishing a public library in Towson and providing the town with its first stop signs and public trash receptacles. During World War II, the club maintained the largest Red Cross unit in the United States.

At 308 Allegheny Avenue is the former Towson High School, which was built in 1907 to replace an existing school across town that was leveled by fire. In 1926, it became the elementary school, after the high school was moved to the large brick building visible to the rear. In 1948, Towson High School moved to its current home on Cedar Avenue. The Baltimore County Office of Personnel currently occupies 308 Allegheny Avenue.

13

One block past Highland Avenue, turn left into the parking lot of the Towson branch of the YMCA. Continue through the parking lot to the opposite entrance on Chesapeake Avenue.

The YMCA may be Towson's most popular community building. It is the largest and busiest YMCA in the Central Maryland region. The YMCA occupies the Kelso House, which was built in 1924 as an orphanage for girls. It moved into the building in 1959, and later expanded with a swimming pool and other facilities. The YMCA's front facade is visible from Chesapeake Avenue.

The spritely brick building on the front lawn of the YMCA is affectionately referred to as "the little red brick building." It emigrated here from its original location on the corner of Washington and Pennsylvania avenues, near the courthouse. There, it served as the law office of Colonel McIntosh, and later as the initial home of Towson National Bank, making it the town's first bank building. It was also used as the headquarters for the Greater Towson Chamber of Commerce. The building escaped demolition in 1968 through a huge civic preservation effort, and appreciates a new lease on life on the YMCA's front lawn. Today, it houses executive offices for the YMCA.

14

Turn left onto Chesapeake Avenue.
Continue on Chesapeake Avenue for one block.

15

Turn right onto Dixie Drive.
Continue on Dixie Drive for one block.

Dixie Drive offers a quiet sanctuary from the frenetic pace of downtown Towson. This is one of several charming Towson neighborhoods that have eluded the renewal process.

16

Turn left onto Georgia Court.
Continue on Georgia Court for one block.

The sprawling building along Georgia Court is the Presbyterian Home of Maryland, which is a retirement community. The elegant middle portion of the Presbyterian Home, including the cupola and portico, was the plaster-over-stone home of Grafton Bosley. Bosley was a local physician who later divorced his medical practice to manage his vast land holdings. He donated land for Odd Fellows Hall on York Road, and later for the courthouse and the city jail. The massive wings of the Presbyterian Home were added to accommodate the retirement center. This fourteen-acre estate was once called "Uplands."

17
Turn left onto Florida Road.
Continue on Florida Road for one block.

Where Florida Road meets Chesapeake Avenue is the Towson Presbyterian Church. This church was erected in 1927, and renovated on four occasions. The church now bears the shape of a quadrangle. Most of Towson's major churches are constructed of stone, unlike other Baltimore suburbs where the congregations seemed to prefer brick.

18
Turn right onto Chesapeake Avenue.
Continue on Chesapeake Avenue for four blocks.

Cross over Bosley Avenue and look right. The stone building one block away is the city jail, which was built at the same time as the courthouse. A more modern county detention facility opened on Kenilworth Avenue in 1957, but the old Towson jail remains in use today. The hanging of prisoners was a public spectacle in old Towson, and usually occurred in the courthouse square. Spectators began gathering in the square the night before. A nearby drugstore stayed open all night, serving the bystanders sandwiches.

Across Bosley is the courthouse square area. The square is the epicenter of Baltimore County's government. Buildings here include courthouses, state office buildings, and ancillary service buildings. Notice on the hill to the left a monument memorializing "officers and families who made the ultimate sacrifice" in the line of duty.

Just past this memorial is the county courthouse. Towson became the county seat in 1854, and the courthouse was constructed in 1857. The limestone for the sturdy walls came from Lime Kiln Bottom, and the marble trim came from the Beaver Dam quarry north of Baltimore City. Major renovations and expansions were made to the courthouse in 1910, 1925, and 1958. Notice how the additions seamlessly match the original unit. The courthouse used to lord it over the village, but now tucks neatly in a fold between Towson's steel-and-glass high-rises.

Wander through the front quadrangle of the courthouse for an impressive view of its facade. Notice the statue of a woman reading to a child. It was designed in 1992 by Susan Luery as a tribute to the school librarians of Baltimore County.

On the front lawn also stands a cannon alongside a pile of fourteen cannon balls. The cannon was captured in Manila Bay, in the Philippines, in 1898, during the Spanish-American War. It was delivered to the port of Baltimore in 1900, and given as a gift to a Towson resident who fought in that battle. Soon after, it was placed in front of the court-house. The cannon balls are welded together for a reason. In the 1920s, a traditional prank was to roll the balls down Chesapeake Avenue on the trolley tracks. Ten balls were lost in this manner.

Immediately across the street from the courthouse, at 405 Washington Avenue, is a vintage bank building. Look up and you will see the old clock situated above the entrance. During World War I, Thomas W. Offutt was president of the Second National Bank, which occupied this building. Offutt noticed that the cannon was pointing directly at his bank. He feared that Germans would fire cannon balls through his building, and vocally protested the aim of its barrel. To appease Offutt, county officials sealed the cannon barrel and pointed it away from his building. Offutt never realized that the cannon balls were three times the diameter of the cannon barrel.

19
Turn right onto Washington Avenue.
Continue on Washington Avenue for two blocks,
until it dead-ends at Towsontown Boulevard.

Towson's post office stands at the corner of Chesapeake and Washington Avenues. The post office opened for business in 1938 to much local fanfare, but a year later it drew the town's ire. A controversial wall mural painted above the tellers' booths by Russian emigré Nicolai Cikovsky was the culprit. It portrayed the metamorphosis of mail delivery in five stages—from Pony Express to air travel. Towson residents complained that the horse appeared to be hopping instead of galloping; that it was not of a breed found in Maryland; that a capital "I" was dotted; and that the connection of the locomotive's drive rods to its axles was inaccurate. The one valid complaint may have been that the mural did not reflect a Maryland flavor. Newspaper editorials called for its removal, but it remains today. Peek in to check it out.

To the left is the Maryland National Guard Armory, which was built around 1935. It is one of the last armory buildings in the nation built in a medieval style. Today it serves as a recruiting station. Directly across the street is a beautiful brick building built in 1926 as headquarters of the Baltimore County police department. The headquarters were relocated to Bosley Avenue in 1960, but the building remains the Towson substation. Notice the glass ball globes with "Police" scripted across. The building is also notable for its green tile roof and swan's neck pediment with a pineapple. The pineapple is a universal welcoming symbol.

20

**Turn right onto Towsontown Boulevard.
Continue on Towsontown Boulevard for one block.**

21

**Turn left onto Burke Avenue. Continue on
Burke Avenue for two blocks, passing beneath
the Towson University pedestrian overpass.**

Towson University is situated along Burke Avenue. The university is the oldest and the second largest in the state (next to the University of Maryland at College Park). It educates about 13,000 undergraduates. The university was founded in 1866 as the State Normal School, which groomed women to be elementary school teachers. Like Goucher College, Towson University's original campus was in downtown Baltimore. The State Normal School, however, was preparing teachers to teach in a rural setting, where the market for teachers was greater. Eventually, college officials deemed it more appropriate to train their teachers in a country setting. The school moved to Towson in 1915, to what was a cow field. It wasn't until after World War II that the curriculum of the college was expanded beyond that of a teacher's college. Over time, the university has also been officially called the State Teachers College at Towson, Towson State College, and Towson State University.

Just before passing beneath the pedestrian overpass, look right up the driveway that leads into campus. The large white house with wrap-around porch is the oldest building on campus. It's known as Glen Esk, and was home to the prominent Nelligan family. The building today serves as the counseling center for Towson University students.

22
Turn right onto York Road.
Continue on York Road for one long block.

The first brick campus building to the right is Newell Hall, which was erected in 1914 as a dormitory and a dining room. It was named for the first principal of the State Normal School. Adjacent to Newell Hall is Richmond Hall, which also serves as a dormitory. Richmond Hall was named for Sarah E. Richmond, who was perhaps the person most influential in moving the State Normal School from downtown Baltimore to its Towson location. She was a teacher, and later a principal, of the school. Richmond gained notoriety by pulling late nights writing and lobbying Congressmen for a better campus. She was known to hover about the state capitol whenever the General Assembly met. Her efforts proved successful, as Towson University now enjoys a scenic perch on Baltimore's outskirts. In 1917, Richmond was named the Dean of Women.

Just past Richmond Hall is Stephens Hall, which is Towson University's most photogenic building. The facade and copper clock tower reflect all the elements deemed worthy of a prestigious institute of higher learning. When the State Normal School moved to Towson in 1915, Stephens Hall served as classrooms, offices, and dormitories. Today it is home to the College of Business and Economics, as well as other departments. It was named for Morse Bates Stephens, a state Superintendent of Education.

23
Turn left onto Aigburth Road.
Continue on Aigburth Road for one long block.

Before turning left onto Aigburth Road, look down York Road. St. Joseph Medical Center stands just out of view. La Paix was a sprawling mansion built in 1885 that once occupied the grounds of a hospital parking lot. It was a summer retreat house for the Turnbull family. F. Scott Fitzgerald stayed at La Paix in 1932 and 1933 while his wife Zelda received psychiatric treatment at St. Joseph and Johns Hopkins Phipp's Clinic. It was here that Fitzgerald penned *Tender Is the Night*. He enjoyed regular visits from H.L. Mencken and T.S. Eliot. Fitzgerald was also known to race his Stutz Bearcat up and down York Road, distracting residents of this quiet community and scattering livestock. A destructive fire at La Paix during the Fitzgeralds' stay was thought to have been set by Zelda. The mansion was razed in 1961.

Soon after the turn onto Aigburth Road is the crest of a hill. The dwelling at the bottom of the hill is the Aigburth mansion. It was home to John E. Owens, who was considered the pre-eminent comedic actor of his day, and thought to be the wealthiest actor of his era. Comparisons are often drawn between Owens and Bob Hope. In their book, *Towson: A Pictorial History of a Maryland Town*, H. George Hahn and Carl Behm III discuss the comedian. Owens bought the 198-acre Rock Spring Farm in 1853, and converted it into what was called Aigburth Vale, considered to be one the era's most gracious estates. Owens continued farming the acreage, but he evidently proved more adept with a script than with a till. His wife once said, "When his friends call, he sets out milk and champagne, with the tearful request that they will take the champagne because it doesn't cost as much." His farming foibles were often the butt of his comedy routines. After Owens' death in 1919, the mansion was converted to a hotel, and the grounds around it groomed with cottages. This is considered to be Towson's first suburban development and was later used as a hospital. The entrance to Towson High School, which occupies Owens' former farmland, is just before the mansion.

24

Turn left onto Maryland Avenue.
Continue on Maryland Avenue for one long block.

25

Turn left onto Burke Avenue.
Continue on Burke Avenue for four short blocks.

26

Turn right onto York Road.
Continue on York Road for about six blocks, to Towson Circle.

York Road is the backbone of Towson, and exists because its gentle slope over difficult terrain allowed horse trains to easily navigate between Baltimore's northern farms and tidewater area. During most of the nineteenth century, York Road was a toll road maintained and operated by the Yorktown Turnpike Company. The word turnpike is derived from the use of "pikes," which were mechanical arms that blocked entrance to the road from other roads until a toll was paid. The original turnpike consisted of a sixty-six-foot right-of-way, which was later widened to one hundred feet. The state of Maryland acquired the pike in 1908, removed the toll booths, and allowed travelers to navigate it for free.

Look right down Towsontown Boulevard. The tiny brick and stone structure about one hundred yards away is the former Baltimore Transit Company substation, which was built in 1947. The building now houses Wilson's Heritage, which is an antique lighting sales and restoration shop.

Just beyond Towsontown Boulevard, two stone abutments flank York Road. They create an ad hoc gateway to Towson's business district. The abutments supported a trestle which carried the former Maryland and Pennsylvania

Railroad over York Road. Public transportation is generally utilitarian in nature, but the "Ma and Pa," as it was affectionately called, transcended that notion. Despite an inefficient and circuitous route between Baltimore and York, Pennsylvania, it was heavily used and became part of Towson's social fabric. Along its seventy-seven-mile course, it crossed over one hundred trestles and bridges and banked about five hundred curves. This was a train engineer's nightmare, since each bridge and curve warrants caution. And the trains crept along at a lumbering twenty miles per hour. Nonetheless, townspeople rode the Ma and Pa for decades. By 1950, driving a car from Baltimore to York was three times quicker than taking the Ma and Pa, and ridership of the railroad began decreasing. One decade later, the train ceased operations and the trestle over York Road was dismantled.

Had Towson's original renewal plan come to full fruition in the 1960s as intended, York Road would be entering a tunnel here instead of proceeding through the heart of the business district. The plan called for York Road to be diverted underground at Chesapeake Avenue and to emerge along Dulaney Valley Road to prevent an overflow of traffic in the downtown district.

At the intersection of Chesapeake Avenue and York Road is Towson's public library, possibly the most contemporary building in town. The library's existence can be traced to the Woman's Club of Towson, which in 1935 established a reading room to the rear of the Odd Fellows Hall. It consisted of about one hundred books in several orange crates. The library subsequently moved to a one-room apartment, and on to a three-room apartment, before settling in to a six-room apartment. It wasn't until 1974 that it was granted this massive, and unique, home. The Towson library today is said to be one of the busiest libraries in the country.

The Odd Fellows Hall, 511 York Road, dates to the mid-nineteenth century. It's one of the oldest Odd Fellows Halls continuously in use in the nation. The 500 block of York Road to the left was ravaged by fire in 1878. Odd Fellows Hall was the only structure on the block left standing. The fire began in a store, and spread quickly when a fifty-pound keg of gunpowder ignited. There was no fire department in Towson at the time, so a local militia composed of both Union and Confederate soldiers was called upon to extinguish the blaze.

Odd Fellows Hall is currently home to the Independent Order of Odd Fellows, which is a fraternal and charitable organization that began in seventeenth-century England to undertake projects to benefit needy people. Back then, it was unusual to carry out such altruistic endeavors, and those who did so were called "Odd Fellows."

Across from Odd Fellows Hall is the Recher Theatre, which is the former Towson Theatre. The exterior of this building has changed little since its premier showing in 1929. For thirty years it was one of the Baltimore area's most popular cinemas. It began to struggle financially in the 1960s when mega-plex theaters assaulted the suburbs. It finally shut down in 1992. Soon after, the building suffered through a stint as a billiards hall; in 1995 it was converted to a rock concert venue and continues to thrive. Ziggy Marley, George Clinton, Johnny Winter, and Macy Gray have performed here.

27

At Towson Circle, follow signs for Dulaney Valley Road. Continue on Dulaney Valley Road past Hecht's department store and Towson Town Center shopping mall.

Beside the Barnes & Noble bookstore is the Wayward Cross memorial, which is often referred to as the soldier's monument. It commemorates those who lost their lives in the Great War.

Barnes & Noble stands at the former site of Hutzler's department store. Hutzler's opened here in 1952 at a time when department stores were the domain of inner cities. The Hutzler family operated several department stores in Baltimore City, but this Towson store was their first suburban outlet. It was built to tap into the post-war suburban flight. Shoppers flocked to the superstore, which at one point was said to have about 275,000 regular customers. Perhaps thanks to the Hutzler family, Towson has always been considered one of Maryland's premier shopping destinations. The Bosley Hotel stood on this site from about 1820 to 1850.

28

**Just past the Sheraton Hotel,
turn right into the main entrance of Goucher College.**

29

**Continue through the security gate.
Turn left into the visitors' parking lot,
which is the end of the hike.**

Suggested Readings

Books

Towson: A Pictorial History of a Maryland Town by Henry George Hahn and Carl Behm III

Baltimore County Panorama by Neal A. Brooks and Richard Parsons

Images of America: Towson and the Villages of Ruxton and Lutherville by Molly O'Donovan and Brooke Gunning

A History of Baltimore County by Neal A. Brooks and Eric G. Rockel

Websites

Goucher College
www.goucher.edu

Towson University
www.towson.edu

Historic Towson, Inc.
www.historictowson.org

Towson Town Center
www.towsontowncenter.com

Ma and Pa Railroad Preservation Society
www.jarrettsville.org/mapa/main.htm

Baltimore County Chamber of Commerce
www.baltimorecountychamber.com

Ellicott City

Frederick Road through historic Ellicott City

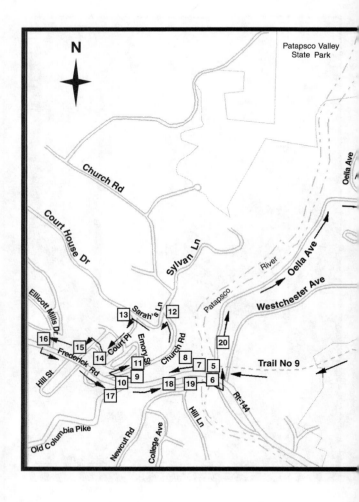

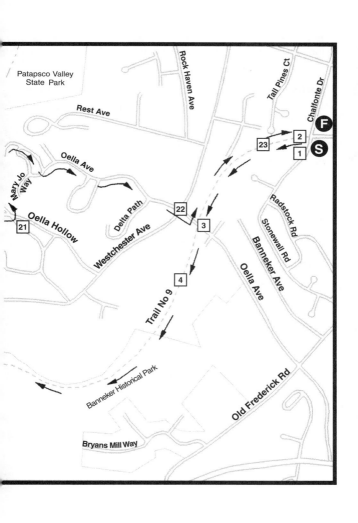

Overview

Distance: Five-and-one-half miles, including several steep hills.

Major attractions: The historic mill towns of Ellicott City and Oella; and the former #9 trolley line right-of-way which has been converted to a paved walking path.

Starting location: The northeast terminus of the #9 trolley trail, which is located where Edmondson Avenue dead-ends at Stonewall Road and Chalfonte Drive.

Directions to start and parking: Take the I-695 beltway to the west side of Baltimore. Take Exit 14, Edmondson Avenue. Go west on Edmondson Avenue, away from Baltimore City (heading outside the beltway). Continue on Edmondson Avenue for about three miles, until it dead-ends at Stonewall Road to the left and Chalfonte Drive to the right. Long-term on-street parking is available along Edmondson Avenue.

Access to eating facilities: Frederick Road through Ellicott City offers plenty of dining opportunities ranging from casual coffee shops to high-end restaurants.

Introduction

When the three Ellicott brothers—John, Joseph, and Andrew—set out in 1771 to establish a vibrant flour mill community, they found the ideal location among the hills of what is now Baltimore and Howard Counties. The Patapsco River provided them ample water to drive their mills, crops from established farms on outlying land provided the grist, and, because of its primitive and rugged nature, the land came cheap. The Ellicotts purchased 700 acres, including four miles of Patapsco River waterfront, for three dollars per acre. On their purchase, they built a tremendous amount of infrastructure, including roads, bridges, houses, stores, and churches. And Ellicott Mills, as it was originally called, took root.

What the Ellicott brothers probably didn't realize was that the mill town they erected closely resembled a European mountain village with outstanding charm that still beams today. Many buildings sit high on rocky crags overlooking town; some are integral with the environment. The views are wonderful, and many creeks weave through the surrounding hills. Most of the mill activity in Ellicott City has waned over time, but it is this European feel that has provided Ellicott City new life. It's been transformed into an artistic community of galleries, coffee shops, bookstores, and antique shops. And yet through this change, it has managed to maintain the historical integrity of the town envisioned and built by the Ellicott brothers, making it one of the state's premier day-trip destinations.

1

**Begin the hike at the northeast terminus of the paved
#9 trolley trail, which is located where Edmondson Avenue
dead-ends at Stonewall Road and Chalfonte Drive.**

2

**Follow the trolley trail downhill toward Ellicott City.
A sign at the trailhead designates the trail as the former
#9 trolley line.**

Frederick Road has, for over two centuries, connected
Baltimore City with Ellicott City. In the late 1800s, electric
trolleys began navigating Frederick Road. The stretch
between Catonsville and Ellicott City offered too steep a
plunge for the trolleys, and was deemed impassable. An alternative route had to be found that offered a more gradual
descent. This trail offered passengers not only a safe ride, but
a delightful one through thick woodland.

Soon after the #9 trolley line ceased operations in 1955,

The Decision That Made a Town

When the Ellicott brothers founded Ellicott Mills in 1771,
tobacco was king. It was grown pervasively on the outlying farms
west to the Monocacy Valley, near present-day Frederick. The
Ellicotts were unimpressed with tobacco as a commodity. They
believed it too quickly depleted the soil of nutrients, rendering it
sterile. They saw profitability in flour mills, and set out to
convince local tobacco farmers to switch their crops to wheat. To
aid their task, the Ellicotts imported chunks of gypsum from
Nova Scotia, which they ground to plaster of paris and provided
to farmers as fertilizer to revitalize their soil. The Ellicotts were
able to convince Charles Carroll, the wealthiest landowner in the
colonies and signer of the Declaration of Independence, to switch
over to wheat. But as part of the deal, they agreed to build a five-
mile-long road from their flour mills to Carroll's farm. This was
the origin of Frederick Road. Carroll successfully made the
switch, and most other farmers followed his cue. The Ellicott
brothers' flour mills quickly became the most productive in
America, churning out over 150 barrels each day.

this right-of-way fell into disrepair, and became a victim of overgrown brush and indiscriminate dumping. In the early 1990s, the right-of-way was reclaimed and paved, and made into a public recreational facility under the jurisdiction of the Baltimore County Department of Recreation and Parks. The trail meanders through dense and tangled woodland interspersed with backyards and meadows. This ecological succession creates edgerow habitat that attracts interesting bird species, which can be seen along the entire mile-and-a-half length of trail into Ellicott City.

As you approach the first road crossing on the trolley trail, notice an unadorned stone church to the right. This is the Mt. Gilboa A.M.E. Church, named for a biblical mountain in Israel. The church was built in 1859 to serve the descendants of a colony of slaves set free decades earlier. It reportedly is the oldest African-American church in the Baltimore area.

3

The #9 trolley trail crosses Oella Avenue in about one-half mile. Continue on the trolley trail past Oella Avenue.

4

The #9 trolley trail crosses a private access road in about one-quarter mile. Continue on the trolley trail past this access road.

Just past where the trolley trail crosses the private access road, it traces the edge of the Benjamin Banneker Historical Park, its namesake's homestead. Banneker is one of history's greatest scientists, and rightfully named the First Black Man of Science. He was born in 1731. His father and grandfather were slaves, and his grandmother was an indentured servant. The Banneker family was able to obtain this 120-acre plot of land by growing tobacco. On his homestead, Benjamin Banneker taught himself complex scientific principles. Among his accomplishments: he built the first clock in the United States, carving the pieces of wood (the clock kept accurate time for fifty years); mastered astronomy to the point of being able to predict eclipses and other celestial activity; played a key role in the survey of Washington, D.C.; and published an annual almanac that garnered international recognition. Banneker is buried at an unknown location on his homestead grounds.

The #9 trolley trail parallels the Cooper Branch watercourse. Near the bottom of the trolley trail is a spectacular cut of granite known as the "deep cut." Its walls are about sixty feet high and were cut in the mid 1800s. It serves as a reminder of the formidable task involved in running trolley lines through such rugged terrain. The 300-foot length of boardwalk slicing through the deep cut was built by at-risk teenagers as part of a federal civil works project.

The imposing white mansion perched above and at the edge of the deep cut is Alhambra, the former estate of John Ellicott. Built in 1859 of Greek Revival and Italianate architecture, the mansion commands a panoramic view of the Patapsco River and surrounding hillsides. Writer Washington Irving, upon viewing Alhambra, said, "I should like nothing better than to have plenty of money to squander on stone and mortar and to build chateaus along the Patapsco with the stone that abounds there." The Patapsco River Valley evoked in Irving memories of his homeland—the Hudson Valley.

Follow this short side trip explained below for a view of Alhambra'a impressive facade. Just before the trolley trail terminates, it runs adjacent to Westchester Avenue for about 100 feet. Cut back onto Westchester Avenue, taking it up a steep incline. In about 100 yards is the front of the magnificent Alhambra mansion. It remains a private residence. Just beyond Alhambra, Westchester Avenue passes high over the deep cut, offering an interesting perspective of the trolley trail. Backtrack the 100 yards down Westchester Avenue to the trolley trail.

5

The #9 trolley trail terminates on a rise along Frederick Road at the east end of Ellicott City's downtown district. Descend the wooden stairs to the left onto the parking lot of The Trolley Stop restaurant, located on Frederick Road.

6

Turn right onto Frederick Road. Continue on Frederick Road toward downtown Ellicott City, staying on the right side of the street.

After leaving the trolley trail, you will notice an eight-story industrial edifice to the left. This was the flour mill owned by Wilkins-Rogers, Inc., which produced the tiny packages of Washington-brand baking products. It also manufactured baking products for the Kenny Rogers Roasters and Boston Market franchises. It was once owned by the Doughnut Corporation of America. The flour mill now sits barren. The Ellicott brothers built their first flour mill on this very site in the late 1700s, and—through flood and fire—a flour mill has stood here since. The present structure was built around 1918.

The gray stone house across Frederick Road from the Wilkins-Rogers plant is the former home of George Ellicott, another member of the founding family. This house was built in 1789, and was originally located across Frederick Road near the Wilkins-Rogers plant. It was relocated here after several losing bouts with floods. A former millrace once cut through what is now the parking lot of Wilkins-Rogers, separating George Ellicott's house from the mill. A pedestrian bridge over the millrace connected Ellicott's house with the mill buildings.

Just before crossing over the Patapsco River, and if the foliage is not too dense, you can see Castle Angelo high on the river's far bank. This Gothic Revival white castle was built in 1831 by French artist Monsieur Samuel Vaughn, and replicates on a smaller scale an actual castle in France that bears the same name. The castle is thought to be named after Michelangelo. At one time, stairs connected the dwelling with the railroad below. It is a private residence today.

The stone piers abutting the Patapsco River to the right supported the railroad trestle that carried the #9 trolley line over the Patapsco River onto Frederick Road through Ellicott City. The trestle was disassembled in 1955 when the trolleys stopped service. A covered bridge once crossed the Patapsco River next to the trestle to accommodate horses and foot travelers, but burned in 1917 and was replaced by the present concrete span.

7

Continue on Frederick Road across the Patapsco River.

Look closely at the Patapsco River bottom. The dark green and black rock strewn across the otherwise gray river bottom is among the oldest exposed rock in the country. According to a 1978 report from the Maryland Geological Survey, the rock derives from the earth's core, and once comprised the floor of an ancient ocean predating the Atlantic Ocean. The rock was deposited here by erosion of an upstream outcrop. In springtime, look for blueback herring and alewife migrating upstream through the riffles; fish passage facilities built on downstream dams have allowed these species to return to their original spawning grounds upstream of Ellicott City.

8

Pass under the Oliver Viaduct onto Ellicott City's main street, which is Frederick Road.

The stone Oliver Viaduct is the unofficial gateway to downtown Ellicott City. This viaduct carries the still-active B&O Railroad over Frederick Road. Two stone arches of the viaduct were removed and replaced with steel girders to allow passage of the trolleys. Just past the viaduct to the right, at 8000 Frederick Road, is a refurbished stone building situated on the Patapsco River floodplain. This building, dating to the late 1700s, was one of several that graced this low-lying ledge, but the only one to survive a devastating flood in 1868. Over time it has been a private residence, a store, and office space.

Most buildings along Frederick Road in Ellicott City—specifically, those that escaped fire and flood—are original and possess historical significance. They are too numerous to discuss individually. In *Historic Ellicott City: A Walking Tour*, Joetta Gramm provides a detailed explanation of Ellicott City's many historic buildings. Information is also available at the Howard County Visitor Information Center, behind the Ellicott City Post Office along Frederick Road, and at the Howard County Historical Society on Park Avenue. As you navigate Frederick Road through the downtown, notice that the older buildings are mostly of simple construction. This simplicity reflects the Quaker upbringing of the Ellicott brothers, who built much of the town.

Just beyond the Oliver Viaduct and to the right is the former Patapsco Hotel, which provided comfort services to rail travelers. The building was converted to an ice house in the early 1900s, and some critical girders were removed to create more storage area for ice blocks. The weakened building eventually collapsed in 1926, and was rebuilt—stone by stone—by Baltimore businessman Owner Pennington.

The tall building adjacent to and uphill from the Patapsco Hotel is a former tavern and opera house where John Wilkes Booth, Abraham Lincoln's assassin, is thought to have begun his short-lived theatrical career. The building served military duty during the Civil War as a prisoner holding site. It has gone by such names as the Opera House, New Town Hall, and Rodey's Amusea.

At 8098 Frederick Road is the former home of the Patapsco Bank, built in 1905. It was said to have a special set-aside room for ladies transacting business there, including writing tables and a fireplace. The large stones built into the building's corners are called quoins. They are supposed to instill a feeling of strength and stability, two qualities expected from a bank. The Patapsco Bank moved here from its original location next door, at 8090 Frederick Road.

Notice the granite outcrop to the right, up Frederick Road from the bank building. This bulwark of rock reveals evidence of the challenge faced by the Ellicotts as they carved a street through such rugged terrain. Closely inspect the rock for drill holes where explosives were inserted for demolition.

9

Continue on Frederick Road past where
Old Columbia Pike enters from the left.

Across from where Old Columbia Pike enters is the former Howard House Hotel. This five-story structure dates to 1840, but many rounds of renovations, including several enlargements, have changed its appearance over time. It once had two stories of wrought-iron balconies. Joetta Gramm, in *Historic Ellicott City: A Walking Tour*, explains that the hotel was built so tight against the steep hillside, that people walking from Frederick Road to the courthouse often used it as a short-cut to climb the hill, which made for good business at the hotel's bar and dining hall. Today, the building is occupied by the Howard House Apartments.

10

Turn right onto Church Road.
Continue uphill on Church Road for two blocks.

The wedge-shaped structure at the intersection of Frederick and Church roads is the former village firehouse, built in 1889. It was Howard County's first fire station, and now serves as a museum. The cupola which contained the fire bell is still intact. Before that time, fires were extinguished by bucket-brigades—a long line of citizens passing leather buckets of water from the Patapsco River to the burning building. The fire station was purposely built on a downhill slope so that the horses could get a running start.

11

Continue on Church Road past where
Emory Street enters from the left.

Look down Emory Street. The stone building with green cupola at the street's end served as Howard County's primary prison from 1878 until the modern facility was built in

Jessup a century later. It's also called Willow Grove, having originally been situated in a glade of trees. The prison is used today as a daytime holding cell.

Just beyond Emory Street, look right far beyond the houses. From the steep hillside across town emerges the spire of St. Paul's Roman Catholic Church. It was in this stone church that in 1914 an unknown baseball slugger named George Herman (Babe) Ruth married a seventeen-year-old waitress named Helen Woodford. Ruth was born and raised in nearby Baltimore City, but was pitching for the Boston Red Sox at the time of his wedding.

Farther along Church Road is a brown guard rail. In fall and winter, this spot provides a postcard vantage of the Patapsco River as it winds through the mill town of Oella. Aside from the striking beauty, notice the large brick industrial building situated along the river. This once housed one of the largest textile mills in the country. The former mill houses are also visible lining the river.

Approaching Sarah's Lane, straight ahead are the ominous ruins of what was once among the finest educational institutions in the United States. The Patapsco Female Institute was often mentioned in the same breath as Harvard and Yale. Many prominent Americans, among them Robert E. Lee, enrolled their daughters there. It operated as a school from 1837 to 1890, and afterwards as a hotel, hospital, nursing home, and theater. Today, the shell is preserved as a historic park.

12
Turn left onto Sarah's Lane.
Continue on Sarah's Lane for one block.

The large mansion along Sarah's Lane is Mount Ida. It was built sometime around 1830 by William Ellicott, and later sold to a prominent judge in town. Today the building is the visitor center for the Patapsco Female Institute Historic Park, where tickets can be purchased to enter the ruins.

13

Turn left onto Court Place. Continue on Court Place for two blocks, until it dead-ends at an unmarked street, which is Court Avenue.

Court Place runs alongside the Howard County courthouse. Construction of the courthouse began in 1841, and was completed in 1843. The building's original facade was along Court Avenue, overlooking Frederick Road. A renovation in 1986 expanded the courthouse and moved the main entrance to the rear parking lot. The courthouse incorporates a combination of classical and Greek architecture.

14

Turn right onto Court Avenue. Wind along Court Avenue for one block.

The stretch of wood-frame buildings along Court Avenue, across from the original entrance to the courthouse, is known as Lawyer's Row. Since their construction in the late nineteenth century, they have been the offices of attorneys frequenting the courthouse.

15

Turn right onto Frederick Road. Continue on Frederick Road for one block, until Ellicott Mills Drive enters from the right.

The Thomas Isaac log cabin is on the northeast corner of Frederick Road's intersection with Ellicott Mills Drive. Dating to 1780, it's the oldest intact residential structure in Ellicott City. The cabin originally stood a few blocks away, but was reassembled at its present location in the 1970s. The diminutive, gable-roofed stone structure behind the log cabin served as Ellicott City's courthouse from 1840 to 1843. Notice how this structure sits at a lower level than the present road grade; this reflects the original elevation of Frederick Road.

Just across Ellicott Mills Drive, notice the gray mill stone lodged upright. This is an actual stone taken from one of the Ellicott brothers' flour mills. The simple white building behind the mill stone, which abuts the stream called Hudson Branch, was one of the forty mills that once dotted the area. The planking where the mill wheel was attached to the building is clearly visible. Notice how the water level of Hudson Branch has declined over time, due mostly to increased water usage.

16

At Ellicott Mills Drive, turn around and backtrack down Frederick Road through downtown Ellicott City.

17

Continue on Frederick Road past where Old Columbia Pike enters from the right.

Tersiguel's is an upscale French restaurant situated at the corner of Forrest Street and Frederick Road. This was once home to Dr. Mordecai Gist Sykes, who was the town's dentist for decades, and mayor from 1889 through 1897. Every two weeks, Dr. Sykes would ride his high-wheeled bicycle to his office in the town of Sykesville, which is located along Route 32 about twenty miles northwest of Ellicott City.

Cross Old Columbia Pike and look uphill to the right. The string of stone duplexes along the pike is known as Tongue Row, and was built in the 1840s as housing for mill workers. Tongue Row is perhaps the most photographed feature of Ellicott City. The row is named for its owner, Ann Tongue, though the spelling has changed over time.

18

Continue on Frederick Road to the historic district's lower area.

The former Caplan's Department Store stands at 8125 Frederick Road. The building is now occupied by Caplan's Antiques. In 1895, the Caplans bought two adjacent buildings here, including one from Sol Davis, who ran a dry goods store. They combined them into an airy department store with large front windows, calling it Ellicott City's Daylight Department Store. According to Joetta Gramm, Davis' son, Meyer, was a prominent orchestra leader in New York City in the 1920s. He came to Ellicott City in 1972 to perform at its bicentennial ball.

Tiber Alley meets Frederick Road just downhill from Caplan's Antiques. The stream flowing beneath buildings along Tiber Alley is Tiber Branch, named after the mighty Tiber River that flows through Rome. Ellicott City, like Rome, is surrounded by seven hills, so Tiber Branch was named accordingly.

The simple stone structure at the bottom of the hill along the railroad tracks is the B&O Railroad Station, which is said to be the first commercial railroad station built in America. The station was built in 1831 at the terminus of the first rail line laid in America—a twelve-mile stretch built by the Baltimore and Ohio Railroad Company connecting Baltimore City with Ellicott City. Its demure style has been replicated in countless small-town rail stations across the country. This station also has the distinction of being the finish line for the legendary Tom Thumb race between a horse-drawn carriage and a steam train. The horse-drawn carriage won because the steam train suffered mechanical problems along the way. The race did, however, usher in the future of mechanical rail travel in America.

The wood shed-like structure attached to the west face of the railroad station, adjacent to Frederick Road, is said to be the first "indoor" outhouse in America. Immediately in front of the railroad station is a stone and brick plaza that is now used for public sitting. This plaza was once the site of regular slave auctions.

Look high while passing beneath the Oliver Viaduct. On a piece of vertical white planking are tick marks indicating the high water levels of various floods that have ravaged Ellicott City. Crane your neck to see the twenty-one-and-a-half-foot high-water mark of the Great Flood of 1868, which killed thirty-six people, swept away thirteen buildings, and damaged almost every house, store, and mill in its path. The deluge caused over $1 million in damage to Ellicott City.

19

Continue on Frederick Road across the Patapsco River. Take the first left onto Oella Avenue.

Walk along Oella Avenue, and notice to the right remnants of former quarry operations. Granite from this mountainside was used to construct most of the stone buildings in Ellicott City and Oella.

20

Continue on Oella Avenue for about one-and-one-half miles. Do not take any roads that fork away from Oella Avenue. Be aware that Oella Avenue takes several sharp turns through the village of Oella. There are few sidewalks along this narrow road, so stay alert and walk facing oncoming traffic.

Fueled by the success of the Ellicott brothers' flour mills, other mills soon emerged along the Patapsco River. The stone buildings atop the first steep hill on Oella Avenue were part of the Ellicott Iron Works that operated in the early 1800s on what was appropriately called Granite Hill. Today some of these stone structures are private residences.

Just past Granite Hill is the secluded community of Oella. Oella took its name from the first woman to spin cotton in the new world (though her true identity was never ascertained). Oella could be the quintessential American mill town. For almost two centuries, the textile mill, once the largest in America, and the adjoining town were inextricably connected. Each gave energy and vitality to the other, and depended on the other for its survival. There were few reasons for townspeople to leave the enclave, and few reasons for outsiders to enter. The town and mill operated practically isolated like this for almost two centuries.

The first hint of the historic village along Oella Avenue is the string of brick duplex mill houses to the right, just beyond the more modern homes. The Union Manufacturing Company, the corporation that originally owned the mill, owned most of the 130 buildings in town as well, and provided houses such as these to its workers.

The former textile mill rises just beyond the row of duplexes. The mill commenced operations in about 1808. It produced woolen fabrics, including the drab green military fabrics deployed in various war efforts. After World War II, America's fashion taste turned to double-knits and synthetics. They no longer clamored for the fine wool products produced at this mill. Conversion to production of the newly desired fabrics would have been too costly for the mill. In 1972, it shut its doors.

The present mill building was built in 1912 after fires destroyed several earlier versions of the mill. Pass the mill building, and notice above the door of the last entrance the following engraving: W.J. Dickey & Sons, established 1838. The Irishman William J. Dickey purchased the mill in 1887 and continued operating it. He had earlier bought a mill town in Baltimore City and renamed it Dickeyville, which still stands on the western border of the city. Today, the mill building, until recently occupied by an array of salons, galleries, boutiques, and antique shops, is being converted to residential dwellings.

The abandoned three-story stone building immediately across the street from the main mill building, perched behind a high stone wall, was the Dutch Hotel, which dated back to about 1812. It also served as an ice cream store and a shoe repair shop.

21

Just past the former textile mill, Oella Avenue cuts left sharply. Continue on Oella Avenue.

After a sharp left, the building immediately to the right is the former village community center, which housed a store, post office, and medical center for villagers. The foundation of this building dates to the early 1800s.

Just ahead is Oella's most distinctive feature. Long Brick Row is a string of over nineteen rowhomes built along a curve of Oella Avenue. A short brick row is located across the street. More residential structures are located high on the hill to the right. Over 100 of the original 130 buildings which historically comprised Oella remain today.

Surprisingly, until the mid-1980s, the town had no public water or sewage facilities. Sewage was discharged into outhouses or ditches and often found its way into the Patapsco River. Furthermore, the town's outhouses were situated too close to its water wells, and the quality of the drinking water was questionable. After years of lobbying, public water and sewage facilities were introduced to Oella in 1984. Most houses received running water for the first time.

22

About three-quarters of a mile past the former textile mill building, Oella Avenue intersects Westchester Avenue. Continue straight on Oella Avenue across the intersection. In about 100 yards, the #9 trolley trail crosses Oella Avenue. Turn left onto the #9 trolley trail.

The Treasure Hunt

Many legends surround the Ellicott City and Oella area, but perhaps none as compelling as the one related to the property of Catonsville Middle School. The school is located at the corner of Edmondson Avenue and Stonewall Road. It is said that somewhere on these grounds a large sum of money was buried—and never found. In 1802, French shipping magnate Jean Champayne fled his native country during a revolution, and bought the 200-acre Windsor estate on which the present-day school is built. He managed to confiscate between $50,000 and $100,000 before he fled. Champayne placed this money in an iron box and buried it in a remote area of his property. He revealed the location only to his servant, swearing him to secrecy. The servant remained loyal to his oath, and only on his deathbed did he reveal that somewhere on the property is buried a generous sum of loot. Treasure hunters for decades have rummaged the property with shovel and metal detector, but to this day the money has not surfaced.

23

Continue on the #9 trolley trail for about one-quarter mile uphill. The trolley trail will terminate at Edmondson Avenue. This hike ends at this terminus of the #9 trolley trail.

Suggested Reading

Books

Historic Ellicott City: A Walking Tour by Joetta Gramm

The Patapsco: Baltimore's River of History by Paul J. Travers

The Ellicotts: Striving for a Holy Community by Alison Ellicott Mylander

Ellicott City, Maryland: Mill Town, U.S.A. by Celia M. Holland

Websites

Howard County Chamber of Commerce
www.howardchamber.com

The Oella Company
www.oellacompany.com

B&O Railroad Station Museum
www.ecbo.org

Frederick

Fountain in Court Square, Frederick

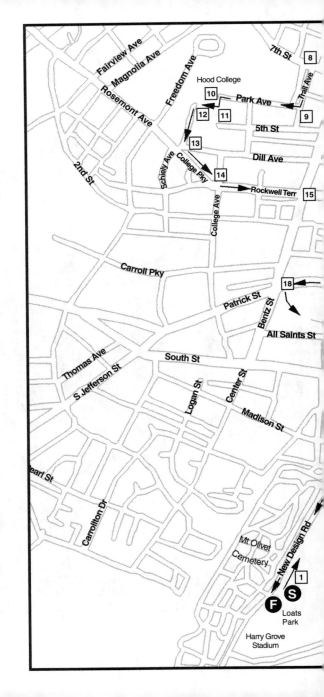

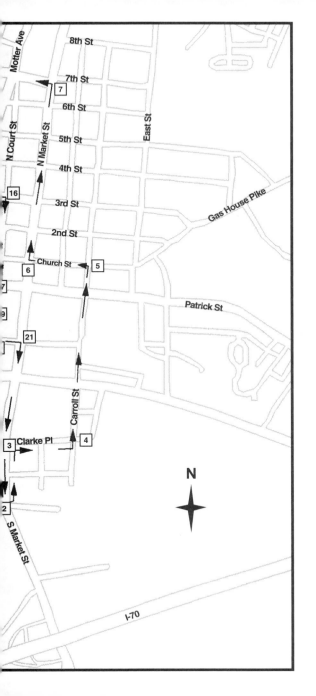

Overview

Distance: Five miles.

Major attractions: Frederick historic district and Hood College.

Starting location: The parking lot of Loats Park, located next to Harry Grove Stadium.

Directions to start and parking: From Baltimore City, take I-70 west toward Frederick. In Frederick, take Exit 54, Market Street. After the exit ramp, turn left onto Market Street, also called Route 355, toward downtown Frederick. Continue on Market Street for about one-half mile. Just before the entrance to Mt. Olivet Cemetery, turn left onto New Design Road. Continue on New Design Road for about one-quarter mile. Park at the far end of the large parking lot to the left, next to Harry Grove Stadium.

Access to eating facilities: Eating establishments on the Frederick Hike are concentrated along Market Street. They include coffee shops, restaurants, and a brew pub.

Introduction

Frederick is said to be Maryland's most historic city. Such a boast is formidable, given that Annapolis has the nation's greatest collection of restored eighteenth-century buildings, and most of Maryland's history has at one time or other filtered through the streets of Baltimore City. What Frederick has done on an unprecedented level, however, is incorporate the historical elements of its city into its daily rhythms. Frederick is not a museum of American history that is to be viewed from behind plate glass. It's more like an ecosystem, where government, commerce, and tourism all commingle with history. Frederick wears its past proudly. Beautiful antiquated buildings are now occupied by interesting shops and restaurants. In the age of wholesale urban exodus, Frederick planners have successfully managed to keep its most treasured institutions—its courts, libraries, schools, government offices, and businesses—downtown in its thirty-three-block historic district, which makes for a wonderful urban hike.

1

Begin the hike in the parking lot of Loats Park, beside Harry Grove Stadium. Cross the parking lot, and turn right onto New Design Road. Continue on New Design Road for about one-quarter mile.

Harry Grove Stadium is home to the Frederick Keys, a minor-league affiliate of the Baltimore Orioles. The Keys played their first game in Harry Grove Stadium in 1990. Funding ran out during construction of the stadium, and then-Mayor Ron Young declared that whoever donated the balance of the funds would be given naming rights to the stadium. The benefactor was M.J. Grove, who named the stadium after his father. Former President George H.W. Bush, an ardent baseball fan and former first baseman for his Yale University team, attended a Keys game here in 1991.

Spanning the west side of New Design Road is the Mt. Olivet Cemetery, which is the resting place of Frederick's most esteemed former citizens. They include Francis Scott Key, who in 1814 penned the lyrics to "The Star Spangled Banner" during Britain's attack on Baltimore's Fort McHenry (though the tune to the national anthem was taken from an English drinking song titled "To Anacreon in Heaven"); Barbara Fritchie, a Union supporter of legendary proportions; and Thomas Johnson, who was Maryland's first governor. About 800 Union and Confederate Civil War soldiers lie here as well. The first person buried in Mt. Olivet Cemetery was sixty-seven-year-old Ann J. Crawford in 1854.

The prominent monument near the cemetery's entrance is the burial crypt of Francis Scott Key. It was designed by Alexander Doyle, a notable New York City sculptor, and dedicated in 1898.

2
Turn left onto Market Street.
Continue on Market Street for two blocks.

The town of Frederick was laid out in 1745 on a 7,000-acre plot of land known as Tasker's Chance. The town is thought to be named for Frederick Calvert, the sixth and final Lord Baltimore. At that time it was part of an expanded Prince George's County. Today, with a population of over 50,000, Frederick is Maryland's second largest incorporated city, behind only Baltimore.

Market Street runs north-south through Frederick's heart, and is one of its primary social and business thoroughfares. It's lined with historic rowhouses, many predating the Civil War. By virtue of its location near the Mason-Dixon Line, Frederick was drawn into the war. Some of the most bloody confrontations happened just outside of town, including the battles of Antietam, Monocacy, and South Mountain. The town itself experienced aggression during the Civil War, when a two-day skirmish broke out that saw Union and Confederate soldiers fighting along Market Street.

Frederick's most tense moment happened in 1864. That's when General Robert E. Lee sent tens of thousands of Confederate troops into town under the command of

General Jubal Early. Upon arrival, Early demanded a ransom of $200,000 from the city, or else his troops would burn Frederick to the ground. The mayor and local businessmen anted up, and the city's beautiful architecture was spared. Historians may remember that Chambersburg, Pennsylvania, was given the same ultimatum, but refused to oblige. The center of that town was burned to the ground.

3

Turn right onto Clarke Place.
Continue on Clarke Place for two blocks.

Clarke Place is one of Frederick's finest residential streets. It's lined with stately Victorian mansions erected before the turn of the last century. The houses were built on farmland owned by Dr. Bradley Tyler. The oldest house on the street is thought to be 104 Clarke Place. Today most remain single-family private dwellings, though some have been subdivided into apartments. Clarke Place was named for a local railroad man, James C. Clarke.

Directly across Clarke Place is the campus of the Maryland School for the Deaf, which was established in 1868. This is Maryland's premier institution for the hearing-impaired. A spectacular five-story brick Victorian building, with three ornate cupolas, once stood on this site. At the request of the state—and much to the chagrin of historic preservationists—it was razed in the 1960s to make room for more modern facilities. In 1931, Helen Keller, subject of the movie *The Miracle Worker*, lectured students at the Maryland School for the Deaf. A prior plan that never came to fruition was to build the Frederick Community College here.

Look for the fountain in the middle of campus. Immediately behind it is a long, stone structure, now enveloped by the school's brick buildings. This is one of Frederick's oldest and most venerable buildings. It's what remains of the Hessian Barracks, which were built to house troops soon after the outbreak of the Revolutionary War. Until then, soldiers were typically quartered in local homes. The barracks soon became used as a military prison for captured Hessian soldiers, who were mercenaries fighting for the British, many of them from Germany. The Hessian prisoners were loosely guarded, and some actually took employment on nearby farms. In fact, a large number of Hessians chose to stay in Frederick following the war's end. This particular site was selected for the Hessian Barracks because the popular Susquehanna Trail passed through the village here, creating a natural meeting spot.

The Hessian Barracks historically served many purposes. During various war efforts, they were either barracks, a prison, or a hospital. They served as the staging area for the Lewis and Clark expedition because of their proximity to the town of Catoctin Furnace, which was considered the gateway to the wilderness. And for a brief spell in the 1840s, they were used as a silk worm cocoonery.

4

Turn left onto Carroll Street.
Continue on Carroll Street for five blocks.

Frederick's historic mill area begins just past South Street. Remnants of former mill buildings line both sides of the street, housing antique markets and a coffee shop. The two structures separated by Carroll Street, but connected by an overpass, were once a grainery that continued operations into the 1950s. Notice the National Park Service's Historic Preservation Training Center, set back from the road, just before the overpass.

The tiny yellow building past the grainery is a former freight terminal for the B&O Railroad. An earlier depot built here in 1831 was purportedly the oldest freight depot in the world. It was torn down in 1911 and replaced with this structure, which is presently vacant.

Carroll Creek, which historically drove the mills, crosses Carroll Street just past the Delaplaine Visual Arts Center. Carroll Creek has been narrowed into a concrete channel with plain paved banks because of the creek's track record of wreaking havoc on downtown during floods. The final straw came in 1976, when seven inches of rain fell on Frederick in

That Which Deceives the Eye

The Community Bridge is a mosaic of illusions. The walls, which appear to be old and weathered stone, are really just smooth concrete. The paint is playing tricks on the eyes. Brush your hands across the surface for proof. People have been observed standing next to the painted stone wall asking where the mural is. An iron gate stands on the bridge's south side. It can't be opened because it's not real. See the painted fountain across from the gate? It looks inviting, doesn't it? So do all the birds that try to land on it. See the ivy along the top of the wall? Painted! Passersby still admonish City Hall for letting so much ivy grow over the Community Bridge. And its most famous icon of imagery is the archangel, on the east face of the bridge. Sure, it looks funky, but the image changes when viewed from different perspectives. The archangel drawing was crafted to look natural when seen from a lower window of the Delaplaine Visual Arts Center. Check out the interpretive sign near the archangel painting for a lesson in the *trompe l'oeil* art style.

sixteen hours, causing a 100-year flood—a deluge so destructive that its chances of happening occur once every 100 years. The city pumped $60 million into the channelization project, which was completed in 1996.

The Delaplaine Visual Arts Center is former home to the Mountain City Mill. The city received the building in 1987 from the Delaplaine family as part of a property trade. In exchange, the Delaplaines received fifteen acres of land on Gambrill Mountain to the west of town.

Just past the Delaplaine Visual Arts Center, take the steps down to Carroll Creek to see one of Frederick's most intriguing attraction. What appears to be a weathered stone bridge adorned with iron gates and fountains is actually a plain concrete bridge painted to look that way. The Community Bridge is an illusion, painted in a style called *trompe l'oeil*, which translates as "that which deceives the eye." The Community Bridge is so named because its artist, William Cochran, incorporated into the mural symbols and imagery contributed from Frederick citizens who were asked the question: What best symbolizes the concept of community? The symbols are discussed on the interpretive sign to the east of the bridge.

Carroll Street intersects Patrick Street just past Carroll Creek. Patrick Street is the heart of Frederick's antique district. The hike does not follow this stretch of Patrick Street, but someone interested in antiques might want to turn left for a brief diversion. The brick structure on the southeast corner of Carroll and Patrick streets is now occupied by the *Frederick News-Post*, the city's daily newspaper. The building was erected in 1910 as the central depot of the city's trolley system. The trolleys entered and left the building through its main bay entrance along Patrick Street. Trolley service connected Frederick with such towns as Braddock Heights, Middletown, Hagerstown, Thurmont, and Jefferson. The *Frederick News-Post* moved here in 1968 from its former office on Court Street.

5
Turn left onto Church Street.
Continue on Church Street for two blocks.

Carroll Street, just beyond Church Street, becomes Chapel Alley in honor of St. John the Evangelist Catholic Church, whose shiny gold steeple bearing a cross is visible above the roofline. The church was built in 1833 by Irish immigrants. Four years later it became the first Catholic Church consecrated in the United States. Most of the essential Catholic hierarchy from across the country attended the ceremony. One hundred years to the day the church was consecrated, lightning struck its steeple. The tower burned, but the remaining structure escaped unharmed.

The Visitation Academy stands behind a high wall on the northeast corner of Carroll and Church streets. The Visitation Academy was started in 1824 by five Sisters from nearby Emmitsburg. The school originally occupied a log cabin on the site. The present building was erected around 1890, and is still in use today. In the late eighteenth century, the grounds of the Visitation Academy were used as a training facility for local militia. The instructor was Robert E. Lee's father.

A beautiful brown Italian Renaissance mansion stands across Church Street from the Frederick County Board of Education building. This was once home to Charles Edward Trail, Frederick's Renaissance man. Trail, primarily an attorney, served on the state Senate, and at one time or other as president of the following organizations: the city's Board of Aldermen, the Farmers and Mechanics National Bank, the Frederick and Pennsylvania Railroad Company, and the board of the Frederick Female Seminary. Trail still found time to be a prolific author and poet, contributing regularly to *Graham's Magazine*, the leading literary periodical of the day. His 1852 mansion is now home to the Keeney and Basford Funeral Home. Notice the stepping stone near the entrance gate, which was used to board carriages.

The Historical Society of Frederick County is located at 24 East Church Street. The structure was built as the private residence of Dr. John Batzell's family in the 1820s, and later occupied by the Loats Orphans Asylum. Orphanages were more numerous in the nineteenth century when illness and war routinely struck parents. The Historical Society moved here in 1959.

The Historical Society of Frederick County is home to the voluminous and highly regarded Englebrecht Diaries, which are considered the premier source of historical information on Frederick (and possibly on small-town life in general). They were written by Jacob Englebrecht, the son of a captured Hessian soldier who stayed in Frederick following his release from the Hessian barracks. Englebrecht was not necessarily a prominent citizen nor a professional writer. He was merely the town's biggest gossip. For decades, Englebrecht jotted down lengthy observations made from the front window of his house on Patrick Street, across from the Barbara Fritchie House.

Across from the Historical Society is the Evangelical Lutheran Church. The twin steeples of this church are the centerpiece of what has come to be known as Frederick's "clustered spires." The church was built in the mid-nineteenth century, replacing previous worship houses on this site. The earliest was made of logs in 1746. Historical photographs in *Frederick: A Pictorial History*, by Nancy F. Whitmore and Timothy L. Cannon, show the sanctuary of the Evangelical Lutheran Church doubling as a hospital for the wounded in the Civil War. Planking was laid across the pew tops, creating an elevated floor where scores of beds were laid out. The 1862 Battle of Antietam resulted in 23,000 casualties, with thousands of the injured shipped to Frederick. An interpretive map of the church's grounds is located to the right of the sanctuary.

Winchester Hall stands at 12 East Church Street, just beyond the Historical Society. This attractive Greek Revival hall was built in 1843, and once housed the Frederick Female Seminary, which became the Woman's College of Frederick. That institution later moved to the northwest edge of the town and was renamed Hood College. Use of Winchester Hall for educational purposes was suspended during the Civil War when it became a makeshift hospital. The hall is named for Hiram Winchester, who built the structure and became the Frederick Female Seminary's first principal. It's now used as city and county government offices.

The three-story brick building facing Market Street, but whose side runs along the south side of Church Street, is Kemp Hall. This building is where the state legislature met in 1861 to decide whether Maryland would remain loyal to, or secede from, the Union. The Senate met on the second floor, and the House of Delegates on the first. Some say that Abraham Lincoln, a staunch Union supporter, suggested that the legislature meet here instead of Annapolis because delegates of the southern Maryland districts—typically Confederate sympathizers—would not be able to make the lengthy journey to Frederick to vote. If this were the strategy, it was successful: Maryland voted to remain in the Union. This sets forth the question: Would Maryland have remained Union-loyal if the vote was held in Annapolis? At the time of the vote, Kemp Hall was known as the German Reformed Building, and was property of the Reformed Church.

6

Turn right onto Market Street.
Continue on Market Street for six blocks.

The building now occupied by the Brewer's Alley brew-pub has a rich and varied history. It was built in 1873 as both Frederick's City Hall and its Opera House. It was the second largest theater in the state at the time. It also contained additional rooms for office space and a farmers' market. The dual-purpose nature of the structure provided ideal opportunity for politicking. Theodore Roosevelt once addressed an audience here, as did William Howard Taft, and a memorial service was held here for William McKinley. From its front steps, abolitionist Frederick Douglass delivered a landmark speech titled "Self-Made Man." The Opera House portion of the building operated primarily as a movie theater from the 1930s through the 1970s. City Hall moved to the former courthouse building on Court Square in 1982. The brewpub is named for a stretch of buildings once located on South Court Street where beer was brewed until 1901.

Market Street is lined with buildings steeped in character and architectural charm. An example is the Professional Building at 228 North Market Street. Also notice the former Frederick Trust Company building on the southeast corner of 3rd and Market streets. The large clock above its main entrance was made by the Self-Winding Clock Company of New York. The liquor store on the northwest corner of 4th and Market streets has a beautiful mansard roof with an unusual cupola.

Where Market Street meets 7th Street is a beautiful, but seemingly misplaced, fountain. This is a vestige of what was once an appealing residential intersection. Beautiful houses surrounded the fountain where businesses now stand. One such three-story mansion with cupola belonged to Union Army Captain Joseph Groff. The fountain was placed here in the early 1800s.

7

Turn left onto 7th Street.
Continue on 7th Street for three blocks.

8

Turn left onto Trail Avenue.
Continue on Trail Avenue for two blocks.

Frederick Memorial Hospital runs along the west side of Trail Avenue. The original section of the hospital is at the far end of the avenue, identified by the more aged brick and the columned entrance with second-story balcony. The Baker Annex is adjacent to and right of the original building. It was added in 1927 at the expense of Joseph Dill Baker on the condition that its first floor be used for the treatment of African-American residents. Until that time, African Americans in Frederick were cared for at an inferior infirmary downtown.

9

Turn right onto Park Avenue. Continue on Park Avenue for three blocks. Continue across Hood Alley and onto the campus of Hood College.

Hood College is Frederick's premier institute of higher education. It was formerly located on East Church Street, in Westminster Hall, and called the Woman's College of Frederick. It moved here in 1914 when benefactor Margaret Scholl Hood provided the school with a handsome endowment and made provisions for the purchase of property. The name was changed to Hood College in her honor. Today, the quiet fifty-acre campus is scattered with beautiful brick Georgian classrooms and towering shade trees. Each building is identified by a white sign on its front lawn. Hood College was historically a women's school, but allowed male commuter students in the early 1970s. The first male student graduated from Hood College in 1973. Today it is coeducational.

10

**One block into the Hood College campus, turn left
onto an unnamed road. Carson Cottage will be to
the left just after the turn. Continue for one block.**

11

**Turn right onto another unnamed road.
Brodbeck Music Hall will be to the right
just after the turn. Continue for one block.**

Brodbeck Music Hall is the only building on campus that
predates the construction of Hood College. It was formerly
called Groff Park, and served as a social hall for German
immigrants. The hall was built in 1897 and enlarged in 1922
after it became part of campus. It now houses Hood College's
music program. Just past Brodbeck Music Hall is Hood
College's most visible structure, Alumnae Hall, punctuated by
four massive columns. The four columns are referred to as
Hope, Opportunity, Obligation, and Democracy.

12

**In front of Alumnae Hall, turn left onto
the main road into campus. Continue on that road for
one block, and exit campus through the brick gate.**

13

**After exiting the Hood College campus, cross over
Dill Avenue to the left and Rosemont Avenue to the right.
Take a diagonal left onto North College Parkway.
Continue on North College Parkway for one block.**

14

**Turn left onto South College Parkway.
After crossing over College Avenue,
South College Parkway becomes Rockwell Terrace.**

Rockwell Terrace is among Frederick's prettiest residential streets. The houses were constructed beginning in 1905.
The development was named for Elihu Hall Rockwell, a

prominent local educator who owned the land on which the development was laid out. Rockwell's house stood on what is now the road through Rockwell Terrace, blocking its connection to 3rd Street. It was removed immediately following his death to allow traffic access to Market Street.

15

Continue on Rockwell Terrace for two blocks, until it meets Bentz Avenue. After Bentz Avenue, Rockwell Terrace becomes 3rd Street. Continue on 3rd Street for one block.

Crossing Bentz Avenue, look right. One block away is a large stone fortress-type building touting a Maryland flag. This is the Maryland National Guard Armory, which was built in 1914, and is now used as a community recreation center. In his book *And All Our Yesterdays*, John W. Ashbury explains how history's most famous illusionist, Harry Houdini, entertained a crowd here in 1924—not with his tricks, but by exposing the secrets behind his and other magicians' illusions. Houdini spent the final years of life revealing tricks of the trade. Following his talk, Houdini did wow the audience by swallowing a large number of needles and several yards of thread, and then removing each needle one at a time—threaded.

16

Turn right onto Court Street.
Continue on Court Street for three blocks.

Just past 2nd Street, Court Street happens upon Court Square. This is the heart of Frederick City's government. The brick building located on the square is the former courthouse, which now serves as Frederick's city hall. It was built in 1862, replacing a building that was gutted by fire. City Hall remains virtually unchanged from its original design. Frederick City moved its government here in 1986—a good thing for historical preservationists, since the alternate plan was to place a retail shopping outlet in the building. This square was where repudiation of the British Stamp Act played out in 1765, and where three Tories convicted of treason during the Revolutionary War were hanged.

Two monuments flank City Hall. To the right of the entrance is the bust of Roger Brooke Taney, who was a chief justice of the Supreme Court. Taney was earlier attorney general and secretary of the treasury under President Andrew Jackson. While Taney was chief justice, he made what is called the most divisive legal decision in history. In the 1857 *Dred Scott v. Sanford* opinion, Taney found that Scott was a slave, and thus was not a citizen of the United States and could not sue in federal court. In this decision, Scott was the first justice to define racially what constitutes a slave. Taney married Francis Scott Key's sister, Ann. To the left is the bust of Thomas Johnson, who was a best friend and confidant of George Washington. In 1777, Johnson was elected the first governor of Maryland.

The tiny brick building directly across from City Hall at 104 North Court Street, is thought to be where Francis Scott Key and Roger Brooke Taney practiced law. The Potts Home, built in 1818, is at 100 North Court Street. This is where

Repudiation Day

The placid nature of Court Square today gives little indication of a tempestuous but poignant moment in history that occurred here centuries ago. In 1765, the British government passed the British Stamp Act, requiring that all official and legal documents in the colonies be written on particular "stamped" paper that could only be bought from the British government. Colonists asserted that this represented a form of taxation, which led to one of history's most heated protests. A raucous crowd in Court Square burned effigies of government officials. One court clerk, John Darnell, immediately complied with the legislation for fear of personal harm from the British. He refused a court order from the colonies to stop using taxed paper, and was arrested. As a result of his trial, twelve judges of the Frederick County Circuit Court issued a unanimous order opposing the British taxation, stating that "all proceedings shall be valid and effectual without the use of stamps." This monumental ruling is thought to be the first defiant act by the colonies aimed at British rule, predating even the Boston Tea Party. Because of this event, March 22, 1765, is known as Repudiation Day.

Frederick's first jail was located. The Ross House is at 105 Council Street, along the north rim of Court Square. General Marquis de Lafayette lodged here in 1824 as a guest of Colonel John McPherson.

Just past Court Square, Court Street crosses Church Street. The block of Church Street to the left is one of the most interesting in the city (though the hike continues straight on Court Street). The attractive Masonic Temple, dedicated in 1902, is identified by the fraternal organization's insignia on the building's pediment. The parking lot beside the Masonic Temple was where the posh Park Hotel, and later the YMCA, once stood.

Adjacent to the east side of the Masonic Temple is the former Independent Fire Company building, which was once home to Maryland's first volunteer fire company. The present building was erected in 1895. The Independent Fire Company moved to Baughman's Lane on the city's west side in 1978. This building is now occupied by a financial business. Notice on the front bay doors the fifteen-foot-by-nine-foot carved glass mural crafted in 1989 by local artist William Cochran. Beyond the fire station is Trinity Chapel. Its tower contains some original planking dating to about 1764, making it the oldest steeple in Maryland. The church was rebuilt in 1880, but parts of the original tower were retained.

Across from the fire station is the Evangelical Reformed Church, which was built in 1848. A plaque on the church proclaims that the Woman's College of Frederick—now Hood College—was founded on this site in 1893. General Stonewall Jackson attended services here in 1862 on the Sunday prior to the Battle of Antietam (history notes, however, that he literally slept through services here).

Look right down Church Street. The former house of Dr. John Tyler stands at 108 West Church Street. Dr. Tyler is renowned for performing the first cataract operation in America. He opened his practice in 1786. The cast-iron dog on his front stoop has a storied past. It was stolen by Confederate soldiers during the Civil War, with the intention of melting the iron into bullets. It was later found at Antietam battlefield intact, and returned to its rightful owner.

At 106 West Church Street, with its tall brick steeple, is the All Saints Episcopal Church. In 1876, during a violent windstorm, a 135-foot-tall steeple toppled onto and crushed a Central National Bank building next door.

17
Turn right onto Patrick Street.
Continue on Patrick Street for one long block.

The former five-story Francis Scott Key Hotel stands on the northeast corner of Court and Patrick streets. It was built in 1923 to accommodate Frederick's growing need for tourist and hostelry facilities. Presidential candidate John F. Kennedy ate lunch here while campaigning in 1960, as did Eleanor Roosevelt in 1933. The Francis Scott Key Hotel thrived for five decades before falling victim to Frederick's suburbanization. Travelers began to prefer the drive-up motels on the outskirts of town to the downtown inns. The Francis Scott Key Hotel closed in 1975 and was converted to the Homewood Retirement Center.

Just before turning right, look left down Patrick Street. The Weinberg Center for the Arts, identified by its Deco marquee, occupies the former Tivoli theater, which opened in 1926 during the era of silent movies. The decorative cinema house featured crystal chandeliers, velvet rocking chairs, mosaic tiles, and marble columns. It was the first theater in Frederick to be air-conditioned. It remained a town landmark for over five decades—not coincidentally, the same five that the Francis Scott Key Hotel, located directly across the street, thrived. The Tivoli succumbed to Carroll Creek's ravaging 100-year flood in 1976, and its famous Wurlitzer organ was found floating in the orchestra pit. It reopened in 1978 as the Weinberg Center for the Arts and is a venue for various performing arts.

The new Frederick County Courthouse stands on the corner of Court and Patrick streets. It was built in 1981 to replace the undersized building on Court Square, now occupied by City Hall. The house of John Hanson originally stood at this site. The original intention was to incorporate Hanson's house into the courthouse, but the house's facade

> ## The Tico Bird
>
> In *And All Our Yesterdays*, John W. Ashbury explains that the silly and ubiquitous Tico birds were made in Frederick, in a factory on Jefferson Street, not far from Carroll Creek. Tico birds were the glass-blown figures that resembled lanky storks, and were half-filled with red liquid. They bobbed up and down in pendulum fashion, as if sipping from a glass. They were also known as bobble birds. Tico birds were a mainstay of novelty shops and five-and-dime stores across the country following World War II. The birds were made by Tico Industries, Inc., an altruistic company that included among its employees many soldiers handicapped from war injuries. Making a Tico bird required a complicated twenty-seven step manufacturing process. Many other manufacturers attempted knock-off copies of the Tico bird, but none with the same quality or rhythm of motion as the original. The Tico plant was tightly guarded to prevent proprietary Tico-bird information from getting into the wrong hands.

was found to be unstable and had to be razed. A replica Hanson House, identified by a tiny plaque near the door, was built to be integral to the new courthouse. Many people do not know that John Hanson was actually elected the first President of the United States in 1781. When the United States consisted of thirteen colonies, they were governed by the Articles of Confederation, which were adopted by the Continental Congress in 1781. That Congress voted John Hanson as President of the United States, and he served a one-year term. George Washington became our first official President of the United States in 1788, when he was voted to that position after ratification of the Constitution, which replaced the Articles of Confederation.

The Barbara Fritchie House is located at 154 West Patrick Street, on the banks of Carroll Creek. This is actually a replica of her original house, which also stood on this site. Barbara Fritchie gained notoriety when, at the age of 95 and while ill, she was said to have defiantly waved her Union flag in front of Confederate troops marching by her house. Her popularity rose to legendary status when John Greenleaf

Whittier immortalized her in a poem, the title being her name. The poem was first published in the October 1863 issue of *Atlantic Monthly*. Fritchie's original house disappeared during the Great Flood of 1868. This replica was constructed in 1928 to satiate the curiosity of tourists drawn here to investigate the subject of Whittier's poem.

Thousands of tourists have visited the Barbara Fritchie House over the past decades, but none as esteemed as Winston Churchill and Franklin Delano Roosevelt, who came here in 1943 at the height of World War II. They, along with a number of cabinet members and advisors, passed through Frederick en route to Camp Shangri-La (now, Camp David), which is located north of Frederick. Their impressive motorcade passed through downtown Frederick, where they had to stop and ask directions to Fritchie's house.

From behind the Barbara Fritchie House, the waters of Carroll Creek emerge from the forty-four-acre Baker Park, visible to the right. The park is where Frederickers play. Its most visible structure is the carillion, a seventy-foot-high stone bell tower that opened in 1941. The original bells for the carillon tower were made in Holland, and their total weight exceeded seven tons. The carillon's bells still toll over the city.

18

Immediately past the Barbara Fritchie House, turn left onto the paved walking path running alongside the creek. Continue on that pathway until the first road crossing.

Along this stretch of Carroll Creek, and facing All Saints Street, once stood a tavern that served as Washington's headquarters. It was here that in 1755, during the French and Indian War, Colonel George Washington met with Benjamin Franklin and General Edward Braddock to plan the attack on Fort Duquesne. Braddock proceeded on to Pittsburgh, where he met his demise. Washington, on the other hand, distinguished himself enough in that campaign to set the course for his future. The tavern where they met was dismantled around 1936.

Barbara Fritchie

Up from the meadows rich with corn,
Clear in the cool September morn,

The clustered spires of Frederick stand
Green-walled by the hills of Maryland.

Round about them orchards sweep,
Apple and peach tree fruited deep,

Fair as the garden of the Lord
To the eyes of the famished rebel horde,

On that pleasant morn of the early fall
When Lee marched over the mountain-wall;

Over the mountains winding down,
Horse and foot, into Frederick town.

Forty flags with their silver stars,
Forty flags with their crimson bars,

Flapped in the morning wind: the sun
Of noon looked down, and saw not one.

Up rose old Barbara Fritchie then,
Bowed with her fourscore years and ten;

Bravest of all in Frederick town,
She took up the flag the men hauled down;

In her attic window the staff she set,
To show that one heart was loyal yet.

Up the street came the rebel tread,
Stonewall Jackson riding ahead.

Under his slouched hat left and right
He glanced; the old flag met his sight.
 "Halt!" -- the dust-brown ranks stood fast.
"Fire!" -- out blazed the rifle-blast.

It shivered the window, pane and sash;
It rent the banner with seam and gash.

Quick, as it fell, from the broken staff
Dame Barbara snatched the silken scarf.

She leaned far out on the window-sill,
And shook it forth with a royal will.

"Shoot, if you must, this old gray head,
But spare your country's flag," she said.

A shade of sadness, a blush of shame,
Over the face of the leader came;

The nobler nature within him stirred
To life at that woman's deed and word;

"Who touches a hair of yon gray head
Dies like a dog! March on!" he said.

All day long through Frederick street
Sounded the tread of marching feet:

All day long that free flag tost
Over the heads of the rebel host.

Ever its torn folds rose and fell
On the loyal winds that loved it well;

And through the hill-gaps sunset light
Shone over it with a warm good-night.

Barbara Fritchie's work is o'er,
And the Rebel rides on his raids no more.

Honor to her! and let a tear
Fall, for her sake, on Stonewall's bier.

Over Barbara Fritchie's grave,
Flag of Freedom and Union, wave!

Peace and order and beauty draw
Round thy symbol of light and law;

And ever the stars above look down
On thy stars below in Frederick town!

19

Turn right onto Court Street.
Continue on Court Street for one block.

20

Turn left onto All Saints Street.
Continue on All Saints Street for one block.

21

Turn right onto Market Street.
Continue on Market Street for about five blocks.

The former B&O Railroad passenger terminal stands on the southeast corner of All Saints and Market streets. This passenger terminal was built in 1854 when the freight depot along Carroll Street became too cramped for passenger services. It contained restrooms and a waiting area—considered a luxury at the time. From a train car at this terminal, Abraham Lincoln addressed a throng of bystanders just before departing Frederick following a brief thirty-five minute visit. Lincoln passed through town after surveying the aftermath at Antietam and South Mountain battlefields. He also addressed a crowd in Court Square.

22

Just past Mt. Olivet Cemetery, turn right onto New Design Road. Continue on New Design Road for about one-quarter mile. The hike ends in the parking lot of Loats Park, next to Harry Grove Stadium.

Suggested Reading

Books

Pictorial History of Frederick, Maryland: The First 250 Years, 1745-1995 by Nancy F. Whitmore, Tom Gorsline, and Timothy L. Cannon

And All Our Yesterdays by John W. Ashbury

Textbook History of Frederick County by Paul P. Gordon and Rita S. Gordon

Mirror on Frederick by Frances A. Randall

Websites

City of Frederick Government
www.cityoffrederick.com

Frederick County Government
www.co.frederick.md.us

Historical Society of Frederick County
www.hsfcinfo.org

Hood College
www.hood.edu

Maryland School for the Deaf
www.msd.edu

The Community Bridge Project
www.bridge.skyline.net

Annapolis

State capitol building, Annapolis

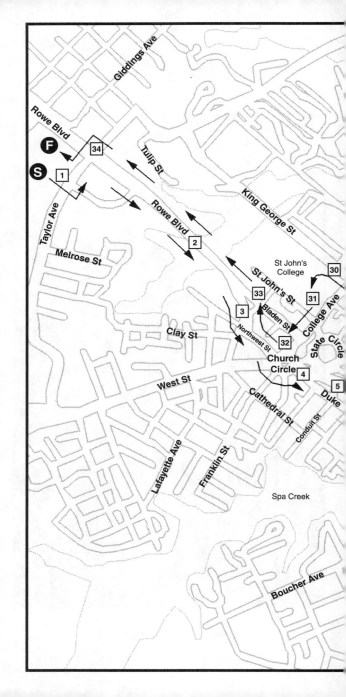

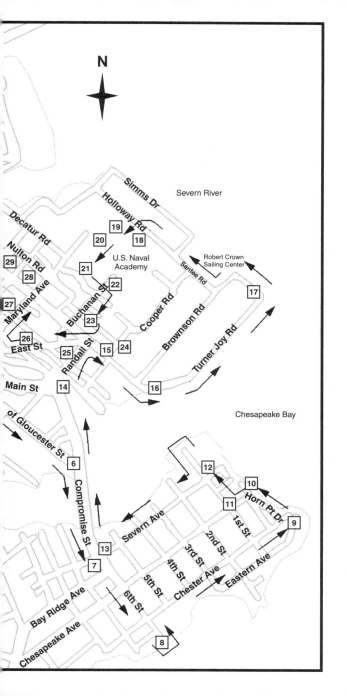

Overview

Distance: Six miles.

Major attractions: Historic Annapolis, Eastport, the U.S. Naval Academy, and St. John's College.

Starting location: The parking lot of Navy-Marine Corps Memorial Stadium. The stadium is located on the south side of Rowe Boulevard, between Farragut Road and Taylor Avenue. Access to the parking lot is from Taylor Avenue. There is presently a flat fee for parking in this lot. Plans are underway to reconfigure the parking lot and switch to an hourly fee schedule. Free on-street parking may be available in the neighborhood across Farragut Road.

Directions to start and parking: From Baltimore, take I-97 south toward Annapolis. Nearing Annapolis, follow signs for Route 50 east. I-97 will eventually merge onto Route 50 east. Stay on Route 50 for about three miles. Take Exit 24, Rowe Boulevard. Go south on Rowe Boulevard toward downtown Annapolis. At the second stoplight, just past the Navy-Marine Corps Memorial Stadium, take a right onto Taylor Avenue. Take a quick right into the parking lot designated Gold. The pay booth is located at the entrance to the lot.

Access to eating facilities: Downtown Annapolis offers a selection of taverns, coffee shops, and fast food restaurants. Eastport offers a handful of more upscale eating establishments, as well as local pubs. There is a snack bar at the Armel-Leftwich Visitor Center of the U.S. Naval Academy.

Introduction

Annapolis was given the gift of three outstanding attractions that draw visitors to its streets. First, it has history. Annapolis has the greatest concentration of eighteenth-century houses in the United States. Fifty structures in Annapolis predate the Revolutionary War, many of them considered the nation's finest examples of colonial Georgian architecture. Annapolis also has the water. Perched on a protected lip of the Chesapeake Bay, Annapolis is a magnet for boaters. On fine days, sailboats and cruisers by the hundreds ply its waters, and in disagreeable weather, they cluster in thickets around its marinas. Annapolis has rightly earned its moniker "The Sailing Capital of the World." And finally, Annapolis has the U.S. Naval Academy, which has an unparalleled combination of beauty, history, and tradition. The academy hosts about one-and-a-half million visitors each year. This hike will explore all three of Annapolis' star attractions, and toss in a side excursion through the less-trodden community of Eastport. Note that this hike can be shortened by over one mile by eliminating the Eastport loop, but doing so would sidestep one of Annapolis' most quaint and beautiful residential communities.

1

Begin the hike in the parking lot of Navy-Marine Corps Memorial Stadium. Follow Taylor Avenue one block to Rowe Boulevard. Turn right onto Rowe Boulevard. Continue on the right side of Rowe Boulevard toward downtown Annapolis.

2

Continue on Rowe Boulevard, across College Creek, into downtown Annapolis. Just past College Creek, and immediately before the Louis L. Goldstein Treasury Building, the road forks. Go right at that fork.

College Creek is a short tributary of the Severn River. Crossing College Creek, look left. The cluster of brick buildings on the far bank of the creek is St. John's College. The Beneficial-

Hodson boathouse, the center for rowing and sailing activity at the college, is visible on the far bank of College Creek.

Rowe Boulevard cuts through a stretch of state office buildings and churches. One of the most attractive is the Louis L. Goldstein Treasury Building, which was built in 1958 during a flurry of state office construction along the boulevard. This treasury building is Georgian Revival in design, so as to replicate the colonial Georgian architectural style pervasive in Annapolis. However, the sheer mass of the treasury building deviates from the traditional Georgian structures.

3

Cross over Calvert Street and veer left onto Northwest Street. Pass between the State Treasury Building to the left, and the Arundel Center to the right. Continue on Northwest Street for one block, until it dead-ends at Church Circle. Turn right onto Church Circle.

The Annapolis Visitor Center is set back from Northwest Street, just before Church Circle. It's an excellent source for information on the city.

Church Circle is one of two circles established as the focal point of Annapolis (the other being State Circle). The Maryland state capital was moved from St. Mary's City to Annapolis in 1694. Governor Francis Nicholson designed the layout of Annapolis, placing a circle on each of the town's two highest points. Within one he built the State House, and within the other, a church. Streets stretch outward from each circle, like spokes on a wagon wheel. These streets allow for wonderful views of the Chesapeake Bay, at the same time drawing eyes to the State House and church. This design replicated the layout of several English towns created by Christopher Wren, and also hints of Versailles in France.

St. Anne's Episcopal Church rises from Church Circle. The present St. Anne's structure was the third church built on this site. The original church was built here in 1704 to accommodate colony parishioners, when church attendance was mandatory. The expanding colony quickly outgrew that church, and it was dismantled and rebuilt to a larger scale.

Fire leveled the second church in 1858 and the present structure was built soon after. The only feature intact today from the original church is the gold ball ornament on the steeple.

Reynold's Tavern, a busy meeting place in colonial Annapolis, stands on Church Circle between West and Franklin streets. The Reynold's Tavern building was built in 1737 for hatmaker Williams Reynold, and was not used as a tavern until 1747. It was later used as a boarding house, a bank, and office space. The tavern provides a fine example of a masonry peculiarity known as all-header bond, where each brick in the building facade is laid with the short end outward. All-header bond was common in colonial Annapolis, but rare elsewhere. Notice the string arch brickwork over the windows.

Immediately past Reynold's Tavern, look down Franklin Street. The Banneker-Douglass Museum is located about one-half block down on the left. The museum occupies the former Mt. Moriah A.M.E. Church, which was chartered in 1803. The present building dates to 1874. It's one of the country's first churches built by freed black slaves. The museum was named for scientist Benjamin Banneker and abolitionist Frederick Douglass, and commemorates African-American history in Annapolis. The building is a fine example of small-scale Victorian-Gothic architecture.

4

Continue walking counter-clockwise around Church Circle. Turn right onto Duke of Gloucester Street. Continue on Duke of Gloucester Street for about five blocks.

The wedge-shaped Maryland Inn stands where Duke of Gloucester Street meets Church Circle. The inn still offers a snug bed and a warm meal, as it did in 1784. The Maryland Inn was the first structure in Annapolis built specifically as a hotel. It was erected on land used by the town drummer, which was Annapolis' equivalent of the town crier. The drummer's mission was to convey information to the townspeople through a series of complex drum beats. The Maryland Inn was for a time known as the King of France

Tavern, to honor the thousands of French soldiers stationed in Annapolis during the Revolutionary War.

Duke of Gloucester Street reveals the hodgepodge of architectural styles employed in colonial Annapolis. Houses along Duke of Gloucester Street are large and small, brick and clapboard, Victorian and Georgian. Two adjacent houses highlight this variety: 199 Duke of Gloucester Street is an early twentieth-century Georgian Revival dwelling, bold and unadorned; 195 Duke of Gloucester Street is nineteenth-century Victorian, sporting a lavish porch, bay area, and mansard roof.

Cross Conduit Street, and look left. The string of six multi-hued rowhouses is known as Rainbow Row. Rainbow Row was an annex to Mann's Hotel, which was the large brick building at the row's end. The rowhouses are now private residences. George Washington lodged at Mann's Hotel when he came to Annapolis in December 1783 to resign his commission as commander-in-chief of the Continental Army.

5

Continue on Duke of Gloucester Street past Conduit Street.

The Maynard-Burgess House is located just past Conduit Street. It was home to several African-American families, among them the Maynards and the Burgesses. A recent archeological investigation conducted by the Historic Annapolis Foundation revealed the historical timeline of this house. The investigation suggested that this house was moved to its present site from elsewhere. The addition of a chimney and conversion of a doorway to a window hinted that this building was at some point converted from a commercial structure to a residential one. Evidence also indicated that a second story was added, probably to accommodate a growing family or families. The Maynard-Burgess House is being restored as a showcase of African-American colonial life.

Across the street from the Maynard-Burgess House is the Annapolis City Hall, which houses the Mayor's office and the council chambers. Annapolis serves three levels of

A Primer in Georgian Architecture

Annapolis is considered the country's premier place to view colonial Georgian-style architecture. Most of the grand mansions in Annapolis are of this architectural type. The Georgian style is bold and simple, characterized by a symmetric floor plan and facade composition. Georgian mansions typically feature a centrally located doorway, often capped with an elaborate transom or cornice. Around the doorway is an orderly pattern of windows. Most other facade details are also symmetric. The style may appear stark when compared to the more lavish Victorian style, but in colonial times it exuded supreme wealth and power. Several of the Georgian mansions in Annapolis are of the five-part design. This is where a central housing unit is flanked by two wing units, each connected to the central unit by a segment called a hyphen. The Georgian architectural style originated from the Roman Palladian style, and became popular in England during the reign of the first four Georges (1715 through 1820), hence its name.

government—city, county, and state. The building was erected around 1766, and used as a social hall before becoming the City Hall in 1870. George Washington frequently attended galas here. The building was gutted by fire during the Civil War, but the infrastructure withstood the blaze and remains today.

Architecturally, Annapolis is most recognized for its brick Georgian-style mansions. The Ridout House at 120 Duke of Gloucester Street is an example of such a house. John Ridout built the house in 1765 for his bride, Mary Ogle, the daughter of Governor Ogle. The street facade employs the all-header bond masonry technique. In *Annapolis: A Walk Through History*, Elizabeth B. Anderson reports that the house remains in the Ridout family today. According to the author, George and Martha Washington were friends of the Ridouts, and visited them often. The Ridouts today supposedly have a nightcap of Martha's that she once left behind. The grounds of the mansion used to extend to the waterfront. The Ridout's carriage house, situated next to the mansion, now serves as a private residence.

Beside the Carriage House is the Three Sisters—three rowhouses that at one time were each occupied by one of Ridout's sisters.

Farther along Duke of Gloucester Street is St Mary's Catholic Church, which was built in 1858. Catholics were persecuted in colonial Annapolis. Catholic worship in public was forbidden. It's believed that the state capital was moved to Annapolis from St. Mary's City in part because many felt St. Mary's City was too rich in Catholic influence. St. Mary's Catholic Church emerged as the primary place of worship for Catholic Annapolitans. Notice the metal stars embedded in the high brick wall just past the church and along Duke of Gloucester Street. These are architectural devices that prevent the wall from collapsing.

6

Duke of Gloucester Street dead-ends at Compromise Street. Turn right onto Compromise Street and cross the drawbridge over Spa Creek.

The Spa Creek waterscape reveals how Annapolis earned its nickname "The Sailing Capital of the World." The forest of boat masts swaying and bobbing in Spa Creek is perhaps Annapolis' grandest landmark. The Annapolis Yacht Club is to the left of Spa Creek, just before the drawbridge. The club originated in 1918, an outgrowth of the Severn River Boat Club, which catered to rowers.

Halfway across the drawbridge, look right and back toward St. Mary's Catholic Church. The three-story brick house in front of Spa Creek is the Carroll House, former home of Charles Carroll, the wealthiest colonist and only Catholic signer of the Declaration of Independence. The house was built between 1725 and 1735. Carroll added a stone block seawall in 1770. Despite being a persecuted Catholic, Carroll managed to become a signer of the Declaration of Independence because of his immense wealth and power. The Carroll family owned almost 50,000 acres in colonial Maryland, including one quarter of Annapolis. After Carroll's death, the house served as lodging for young men seeking the priesthood, and for other church purposes.

Maryland had four signers of the Declaration of Independence: Carroll, Thomas Stone, Samuel Chase, and William Paca. Maryland is the only state where the houses of all its signers remain intact.

7

After the Spa Creek drawbridge, Compromise Street becomes Sixth Street. Continue on Sixth Street for four blocks until it dead-ends at the waterfront.

Eastport is the community on the east side of the Spa Creek drawbridge. It's an eight-block-by-four-block peninsula jutting into the Chesapeake Bay between Spa Creek and Back Creek. Eastport was once an independent community, but has since been annexed to the city of Annapolis. True to its roots, Eastport harbors much of the region's maritime business, including boat builders, sailmakers, boat brokers, marinas, marine supply stores, and marine insurance dealers. These businesses skirt the waterfront of the peninsula, and a sleepy neighborhood thrives within. Many of these businesses are visible from the drawbridge. Few tourists cross the bridge into Eastport.

Sixth Street terminates at the Back Creek waterfront, affording wonderful views of the tributary and of the Chesapeake Bay. Here is affirmation that Annapolis' extensive boating community is not the sole possession of Spa Creek. Boats in Back Creek are sometimes so thickly clustered, they obscure views of the water.

8

Backtrack one block to Chester Avenue. Turn right onto Chester Avenue. Continue on Chester Avenue for six blocks.

Along Chester Avenue, look right for interesting views of Back Creek, the Chesapeake Bay, and various waterfront parks and marinas. Eastport is primarily a residential community with the occasional pub and coffee shop. Café Gurus, at the corner of Chester Avenue and Second Street, presents an ideal rest break away from the din of downtown Annapolis.

9

Chester Avenue dead-ends at Horn Point Drive, in front of the Horn Point Courts community. Turn left onto Horn Point Drive. Continue on Horn Point Drive for one block.

10

**Turn left onto Chesapeake Avenue.
Continue on Chesapeake Avenue for one block.**

Where Horn Point Drive dead-ends at Chesapeake Avenue, Fort Horn Street-End Park is immediately to the right. This park provides a clear sight line to the Severn River's confluence with the Chesapeake Bay. On a clear day, the Chesapeake Bay Bridge is visible from here. The bridge is 4.3 miles long and serves as the only link between Maryland's more populated Western Shore and the more tranquil Eastern Shore. The three prominent towers in the foreground belong to the U.S. Naval Ship Research and Development Center.

Fort Horn Point occupied the tip of Eastport Peninsula until after the War of 1812. It not only protected Annapolis from British attack, but served to stem illegal trade in and out of the harbor. The actual location of Fort Horn Point is identified on the sign at Fort Horn Street-End Park. Notice the outstanding views offered to residences of the waterfront houses and condominium units that line the shore to the right.

11

Turn right onto First Street. Continue on First Street for two blocks, until it dead-ends at the waterfront.

One-half block down First Street, Jeremy's Way enters from the right. The unit of ten rowhouses on Jeremy's Way is known as Murphy's Row, named after Charles James Murphy, who built them in 1888. The dwellings housed workers at Murphy's now-defunct Annapolis Glass Works factory, which made glass, pottery, and ceramics. Today, Murphy's Row serves as private residences. Murphy is responsible for the naming of Eastport. When the community was officially considered a town, a post office was placed in one of Murphy's rowhouses. Needing a name for the community, Murphy suggested that of his hometown—Eastport, Maine.

Eastport House Bed and Breakfast is on the southwest corner of First Street and Severn Avenue. This is the oldest house on Eastport, built in the 1860s as a farmhouse. It later served as a schoolhouse.

The end of First Street, at Linhardt-Russell Street-End Park, reveals a postcard vantage of the historic district of Annapolis and the U. S. Naval Academy. The State House dome is visible to the left, and the white-bricked, green-roofed buildings of the Naval Academy sprawl to the right. The spectacular green dome emerging from the Naval Academy grounds is the Chapel. Much of the boat-building in colonial Annapolis occurred along the Eastport waterfront centered around this location.

12

Backtrack one block on First Street. Turn right onto Severn Avenue. Continue on Severn Avenue for five blocks.

On the northwest corner of Severn Avenue and Second Street is the former location of Murphy's Annapolis Glass Works factory. This was once the largest non-maritime business in Eastport. A gray formstone building now stands where the factory office was situated. The Annapolis Glass Works factory later became a slaughterhouse and sausage factory. In 1920, the grounds were converted to the largest boatyard in Eastport.

13

Turn right onto Sixth Street. After the Spa Creek drawbridge, Sixth Street becomes Compromise Street. Follow Compromise Street toward the historic district.

The Museum Store, run by the Historic Annapolis Foundation, stands at 77 Main Street along the city dock. This building is the former Victualling Warehouse, where supplies were stored awaiting transport to troops during the Revolutionary War. Victuals was a term used in the 1700s to describe foodstuff. The building has been restored to acknowledge the vast number of warehouse buildings that historically surrounded this waterfront. During colonial times, tobacco was a key Maryland crop. Much of it was exported in hogsheads (barrels) from Annapolis, necessitating buildings like the Victualling Warehouse.

Just past the Museum Store, Main Street angles off Compromise Avenue to the left. Although Main Street is not included in this hike, its shops and galleries present an interesting browsing diversion.

The hub of present-day social activity in Annapolis is along its city dock. It's where revelers come on weekends to eat and drink and watch impressive yachts cruise the waters of "Ego Alley." Ego Alley is the sliver of water leading from Spa Creek to the Market House, and is so named because tight-fitting yachts like to strut their stuff here. Tour boats and charter ships operate from this area. A summer outdoor concert series is held here, as well as the largest boat show in the world each fall.

At the foot of the waterfront, on the plaza near the Market House, is the statue of a man reading to three children. This is the Kunta Kinte Memorial. Kunta Kinte was the slave immortalized in Alex Haley's book *Roots*. In his research, Haley learned that Kunta Kinte, an ancestor of his, was brought to Annapolis in 1770 on the British ship *Lord Lignoir*, and sold into slavery. The monument commemorates Kunta Kinte, and "all others who came to these shores in bondage and who by their toil, character, and ceaseless struggle for freedom have helped to make these United States."

The low-slung building at the water's end, directly across Randall Street, is the Market House. A market has stood in this general vicinity since the early 1700s, but this particular market building was erected in 1858. The Market House provides a convenient rest stop, and the perfect spot to purchase a drink and snack.

A traffic circle stands at the intersection of Compromise and Main Streets. The circle was conceived of in 1885 as a park with an equestrian statue, but construction was never completed. A fountain was later planned there to commemorate the 200th anniversary of Annapolis receiving its city charter, but lack of funding prevented that project's completion as well. A gas pumping station was placed there after World War I, but was removed in the 1970s during harbor revitalization. It has since reverted to a small park where the flags of Maryland and the United States are flown.

14

Continue on Compromise Street to the city dock. In front of the Market House, turn right onto Randall Street. Continue on Randall Street for three blocks.

Located just past the Market House, Middleton Tavern remains an Annapolis tradition. The tavern is thought to have been built around 1750 as an inn for the seafaring. George Washington, Thomas Jefferson, Benjamin Franklin, and James Monroe are among the list of dignitaries that bent elbows at Middleton Tavern. The building has survived a series of fires and renovations to secure its long-standing position as a premier watering hole in Annapolis. Annapolis was considered a party town, even in colonial times. New England had the Puritans, and Philadelphia had the Quakers. Annapolis, on the other hand, had taverns and galas and even horse racing. Perhaps that's why so many notable statesmen frequently visited here.

Just past Middleton Tavern, Randall Street crosses Prince George Street. On the far right-hand side of that intersection is a three-story, white wood-frame house. Next door, at 130 Prince George Street, is a cream-colored clapboard house with green shutters. This is the Sands House, believed to be the oldest structure standing in Annapolis today. The Sands House was built in the late 1600s by Evan Jones, who was a tavern-owner and alderman for Annapolis. In 1768, the house was sold to John Sands, a mariner and sailmaker, and remained in the family for generations.

15

Randall Street dead-ends at King George Street. Turn right onto King George Street. Pass through Gate One onto the grounds of the U.S. Naval Academy. Continue on King George Street for two blocks.

The U.S. Naval Academy is a spectacular institution steeped in history and tradition. The carefully manicured grounds are strewn with monuments, memorials, plaques, and interesting relics like torpedoes and aircraft. An entire day of exploration is necessary to do the Naval Academy justice. This hike will only cover a portion of the grounds. If a more thorough excursion of the academy is desired, guided walking tours depart hourly from the Armel-Leftwich Visitor Center. Each tour is about ninety minutes, which includes a twelve-minute video presentation.

The Naval Academy was established in 1845 on the grounds of what was once Fort Severn. The original academy occupied about ten acres, but has since expanded to over two hundred. It serves about 4,000 midshipmen at any one time, and employs over 600 faculty members, split between civilian and enlisted. The education is free to midshipmen, but each graduate is required to serve at least a five-year military commitment.

Just through the gate, the Halsey Field House is to the right. This is the training facility for many of the Naval Academy athletic teams, and where NBA all-star center David Robinson nurtured his collegiate basketball career. The Armel-Leftwich Visitor Center is integral to the east side of the field house. This center opened in 1995 during the Naval Academy's 150th anniversary, and offers excellent vantages of Annapolis' harbor and the Chesapeake Bay. The Armel-Leftwich Visitor Center contains a snack bar and a shop where Naval Academy apparel can be purchased. Immediately across King George Street from the visitor center is Lejeune Hall, which houses an Olympic-sized swimming and diving pool, and wrestling facilities. The Naval Academy's athletic hall of fame occupies the second-floor hallways of Lejeune Hall. Just beyond is Ricketts Hall, which houses the Naval Academy's athletic offices, and serves as a locker room and training quarters for the football team.

16

Just past the Armel-Leftwich Visitor Center, wrap left around the waterfront on Turner Joy Road, following the seawall.

Though the Boston Tea Party garners most discussion in history books, a similar occurrence, known as the Peggy Stewart Tea Party, happened just off this seawall. In the late eighteenth century, during a period of social unrest in Annapolis, Anthony Stewart's ship *The Peggy Stewart*, named for his wife, arrived from England with a cargo load of tea. Tea at that time was deemed taxable by the British, to the protests of colonists. Stewart paid the duty, and when he did, civil discontent erupted into riots. For paying the tea tax, the rioters threatened to burn Stewart's ship, house, and warehouses, and to burn an effigy of Stewart. Stewart played dumb, asserting that he was unaware his cargo included tea. A compromise was reached. It called for Stewart to run his ship aground, and burn it to the waterline. He did so just beyond this seawall.

Eastport is visible about 200 yards across the inlet of Spa Creek. This location affords an interesting view of the various maritime industries that line its shores.

Halfway down Turner Joy Road, along the seawall, stop for a moment. On a clear day, Maryland's Eastern Shore is visible through the gap between Eastport and the towered grounds of the naval research center. A useful skill for navy personnel is being able to estimate distances across open water. In this case, it's 7.5 miles from this point to Maryland's Eastern Shore.

17

Continue wrapping around the waterfront, past the Robert Crown Sailing Center, and around the Santee Basin. Walk straight on Santee Road, along the basin.

Turner Joy Road follows the seawall to where the Severn River meets the Chesapeake Bay. This is a prime spot to watch boats of all sizes muck about. Watch for Naval

Academy vessels embarking on training missions, as well as sporting events from the Robert Crown Sailing Center, which is also home to the Intercollegiate Sailing Hall of Fame. The Severn River snakes through Anne Arundel County and is lined with spectacular mansions and waterfront developments. The protected harbor where vessels are typically docked is Santee Basin.

18

Continue on Santee Road to just past Santee Basin. Luce Hall is on the left. Just past Luce Hall, turn left into a parking lot. Cross the parking lot, and move right behind Ingram Field, the blue outdoor track. Follow the high wall behind the track, and walk up the flight of stairs that divides two identical buildings. Emerge on Radford Terrace, which separates Michelson Hall and Chauvenet Hall.

Michelson and Chauvenet halls house the Math and Science Division of the Naval Academy. Albert Michelson was a faculty member who in 1873 became the first American scientist to win the Nobel Prize. He did so for measuring the speed of light. The line of sight that he used is indicated by a series of metal discs set into Radford Terrace.

19

Move off Radford Terrace and continue on the brick pathway toward the Chapel. Pass the Mexican War Monument.

The Mexican War Monument, with its four outward-pointing cannons, commemorates the four Naval Academy graduates who died at Vera Cruz in 1846 and 1847. Built in 1848, it was the first monument erected on the academy's grounds. While at the Mexican War Monument and facing the Chapel, look left toward mammoth Bancroft Hall, which is the world's largest dormitory. "Mother B," as it is affectionately called, is home to the entire brigade of 4,000 midshipmen. The edifice comprises thirty-three acres of floor space and contains five miles of hallways. Drop in to the main entrance of Bancroft Hall. Just beyond a spectacular entry foyer is Memorial Hall, which honors all graduates of the Naval Academy who lost their lives in battle.

Directly in front of Bancroft Hall is Tecumseh Court, where noon meal formations occur. The bronzed statue keeping a watchful eye over the court is Tecumseh. The original Tecumseh was a wooden statue of Tamanend, a Delaware Indian warrior chief. It graced the battleship USS *Delaware* and was retrieved from the wreckage of that ship. In 1891, the wooden statue was cast in bronze for preservation. Midshipmen worship this "God of the Passing Grade" with offerings of pennies as they head to exams. The beleaguered Indian chief also receives a fresh coat of war paint before important football games.

Just past the Mexican War Memorial and to the right is the Herndon Monument, named after Commander W.L. Herndon, who in 1857 was the first person to explore the Amazon River to its headwaters. This obelisk holds special significance for midshipmen. During Commissioning Week, plebes stage the Herndon climb. The monument is smeared with hundreds of pounds of lard. Plebes must scale the twenty-one-foot monument by forming a human pyramid, and replace a "dixie cup," or plebe cover, on top with an upperclassman's cap. According to tradition, the plebe who replaces the cap will become the class's first admiral.

To the left just before the chapel is the Zimmerman Bandstand, named for Charles A. Zimmerman. Zimmerman was a former bandmaster of the Naval Academy and composer of the naval theme "Anchors Aweigh."

20
Walk straight ahead to the main entrance of the Chapel.

The Chapel was completed in 1904 on the academy's highest point. It's open to the public if not in use, and well worth the stopover. Many of the elaborate stained glass windows were made at the Tiffany studios, and some convey tales of naval adventures. Notice the twenty-two-foot sculpted iron doors at the entrance. The remains of John Paul Jones, considered to be the U.S. Navy's first hero, are encrypted in the Chapel's basement. The nondenominational Chapel is nicknamed the "Cathedral of the Navy."

21

In front of the Chapel, turn left.
Continue on this drive for one block.

Just past the Chapel is the Buchanan House, which is home to the Naval Academy's superintendent. Next to the White House in Washington, D.C., Buchanan House is said to play host to the greatest number of visiting dignitaries, royalty, and foreign heads-of-state.

22

Turn right onto Buchanan Road.
Continue on Buchanan Road for one block.

Across from the driveway entrance to Buchanan House, and set back from Buchanan Road, is Dahlgren Hall, which hosts academy social functions, and contains an ice rink and a café open to the public. Dahlgren Hall is named for Rear Admiral John A. Dahlgren, who invented what is known as the smooth-bore cannon. The barrel of this cannon was designed such that the thickness of the barrel wall varied to match the differences in internal pressure caused by a cannon ball being fired.

23

Turn left onto Porter Road.
Continue on Porter Road for one block.

The succession of neatly maintained homes along Porter Road is known as Captain's Row, home to many of the academy's department heads and high-level personnel.

24

Turn right onto Cooper Road. Continue on Cooper Road for one block, and turn right onto King George Street. Proceed on King George Street through Gate One and off the grounds of the Naval Academy. At the first intersection, take a left diagonal onto East Street, which heads toward the State House.

The Waterwitch Fire Station is one block to the left. It's thought to be the only fire station in the world designed in the Tuscan style. Just past the fire station, at 162 Prince George Street, is the former St. Anne's Church. The church building was built sometime after 1868. From 1918 to 1962 it served as the Kneseth Israel Synagoue. Notice the decorative brickwork along East Street. Until recently, the Waterwitch Fire Station and St. Anne's Church building served as headquarters for the Chesapeake Bay Foundation, an advocacy organization established to preserve the bay.

Directly across the street from the St. Anne's Church is an outstanding example of the five-part colonial Georgian architectural style. Construction of the Brice House began in 1767 by James Brice, who later became mayor of Annapolis and acting governor of Maryland. The layout is typical of five-part construction: the kitchen house is to the right, the carriage house to the left. Notice the robust sixty-foot-high chimney. The walls of the Brice House range from three to six feet thick. The house appropriately serves as headquarters for the International Masonry Institute.

25

Continue on East Street past Prince George Street.

Cross Prince George Street, and look right. The noble brick dwelling five houses away is the William Paca House and Garden. This five-part Georgian mansion is considered among the most elegant landmarks in Annapolis. It was completed around 1764 for William Paca, a signer of the Declaration of Independence. The house was the first five-part mansion built in Annapolis. The thirty-seven rooms were spectacularly adorned, but its jewel was the two-acre garden in back, complete with terraces, a stream, fountains, a pond, and an Oriental bridge. Finely sculpted gardens in colonial times were an indication of refinement and prestige, and Paca's garden was considered among the best. Annapolis was once referred to as the "Athens of the Americas" because of its abundance of wealth, culture, and influence.

Unfortunately, in the early 1900s, the house and property were sold to a commercial enterprise that built the 200-room Carvel Hall hotel on top of the garden. It wasn't until 1965 that the blunder was reversed. The Historic Annapolis Foundation purchased the property after the hotel was razed, and through the use of archeological surveys, returned the garden to its original state. The house and garden are open for tours.

Continue on East Street toward the State House. Pickney and Fleet streets enter from the left. These streets are lined with tiny rowhouses, many of which lodged soldiers during the Revolutionary War.

26

East Street dead-ends at State Circle. Turn right onto State Circle. Continue on State Circle for one block.

By the virtue of its high perch, the State House is visible from most anywhere in the historic district. The present State House building, the third on the site, was built in 1771, and is the oldest active State House in the nation. It was here in 1783 that George Washington tendered his resignation as commander-in-chief of the Continental Army. A year later, the Treaty of Paris was signed here, signifying the end of the Revolutionary War. The Continental Congress met here from November 1783 through August 1784, making Annapolis the national capital over that stretch. The dome is considered an architectural masterpiece, constructed entirely of wood without the use of iron nails. It's thought that a lightning rod atop the State House dome was placed there centuries ago as a political statement. Benjamin Franklin had formulated his theory on electricity, but the British Empire remained skeptical. The lightning rod paid homage to Franklin and defied the British.

The Old Treasury Building hunches to the east of the State House. Built in 1735, this building is the oldest public structure still standing in Annapolis. It was made to accommodate the dispersion of paper money throughout the colony. Beforehand, tobacco and iron coins served as currency.

Johnson's haberdashery is at the corner of State Circle and Maryland Avenue. On the State Circle wall of the shop is a fascinating historical perspective of the business.

27

Turn right onto Maryland Avenue. Continue on Maryland Avenue for two blocks.

Maryland Avenue was not only the most fashionable residential street in eighteenth-century Annapolis, but a busy commercial center as well. Today, it's still lined with specialty shops, boutiques, galleries, and coffee shops.

The immaculate Hammond-Harwood House is to the right just before King George Street. The Hammond-Harwood House is considered the finest example of colonial Georgian architecture in the country; one of the finest medium-sized homes in the world; and features the finest wood-carved doorway from the colonial era. It's the seminal work of Annapolis architect William Buckland. Today, the original appearance of Hammond-Harwood House remains surprisingly intact. The only modifications since 1774 have been a new roof, some window replacements, and a few coats of paint. The house has come to signify the sophisticated lifestyle of colonial Annapolis. Mathias Hammond, the original owner of the house, like so many other wealthy Annapolitans, was a plantation owner. At one point, Henry Ford tried to purchase the Hammond-Harwood House and move it to his estate in Michigan—brick by brick. His proposal was rejected. The Hammond-Harwood House is now a public museum.

Across the street from the Hammond-Harwood House is another William Buckland masterpiece—the Chase-Lloyd House. Samuel Chase, a Supreme Court justice and signer of the Declaration of Independence, commissioned the house to be built in 1769. Due to financial problems, he sold it to Edward Lloyd IV of Wye Plantation before completion. Lloyd's youngest daughter married Francis Scott Key, who penned "The Star Spangled Banner." The house is open for tours.

28

Turn left onto King George Street.
Continue on King George Street for one block.

29

Turn left onto College Avenue.

The campus of St. John's College is to the right. St. John's College was founded in 1696 as the King William's School, making it the third oldest institution of higher learning in the nation behind Harvard University and the College of William and Mary. Its distinctive liberal curriculum centers around the "great books," which are considered the classic works of western civilization. It was the first institution of higher education in the United States to prohibit religious discrimination. Francis Scott Key attended St. John's College.

30

Just after turning left onto College Avenue, take a quick right onto the walkway that slices across campus.

Chase-Stone Hall is a dormitory named after Samuel Chase and Thomas Stone, two Marylanders who signed the Declaration of Independence. The hall originally served as living quarters for the college's president and vice president. In front and to the left of Chase-Stone Hall was the site of the Liberty Tree, which after four centuries met its demise by Hurricane Floyd in 1999. To the left of Chase-Stone Hall is Pickney Hall, another dormitory. Both dormitories date to the nineteenth century.

McDowell Hall, to the left of Pickney Hall, looms as the centerpiece of St. John's College. McDowell Hall was visualized by Governor Thomas Bladen as the Governor's Mansion, and construction began in 1742. Before completion, the Maryland legislature deemed the building too extravagant and costly, and halted funding. It stood roofless for fifty years, earning the nickname "Bladen's Folly." It was finally capped off in 1792 for use by the college. The exterior of McDowell Hall has not been modified since its completion, with the exception of a porch added to the east entrance. Today McDowell Hall serves as classrooms.

When in front of McDowell Hall, look toward College Avenue. Near the street is a cast-iron model of the Liberty Bell. This is one of forty-eight Liberty Bell replicas cast in 1950 by the U.S. Department of Treasury to promote the sale of defense bonds.

31

Past McDowell Hall, take the diagonal walkway back to College Avenue, toward the State House. Turn right onto College Avenue. Continue on College Avenue for two blocks.

Just past the State House is the Government House, which is the residence of Maryland's governor. Though built in 1866 in Victorian style, the house was appropriately renovated to the five-part colonial Georgian style in 1935. Porches and a mansard roof were removed, and wings and hyphens were added. The rear of the house faces College Street.

32

**Turn right onto Northwest Street.
Continue on Northwest Street for one block.**

33

Just past the Louis L. Goldstein Treasury Building, cross over Calvert Street and veer right onto the road leading to Rowe Boulevard. Turn left onto Rowe Boulevard. Stay to the left on Rowe Boulevard, facing traffic.

34

Just before Navy-Marine Corps Memorial Stadium, turn left onto Taylor Avenue. Continue on Taylor Avenue for one block. Turn right into the Gold parking lot of the Navy-Marine Corps Memorial Stadium, which is the end of the hike.

Suggested Reading

Books

Annapolis: A Walk Through History by Elizabeth B. Anderson

Annapolis: The Guidebook by Katie Moose

Builders of Annapolis by Norman K. Risjord

Annapolis Pasts: Historical Archeology in Annapolis, Maryland edited by Paula A. Shackel; Paul R. Mullins, and Mark S. Warner

Websites

General Information Page
www.covesoft.com/annapolis

Hometown Annapolis
www.hometownannapolis.com

Visit Annapolis
visit-annapolis.org

City of Annapolis
www.ci.annapolis.md.us

U.S. Naval Academy
www.usna.edu

St. John's College
www.sjca.edu

Historic Annapolis Foundation
www.annapolis.org

Acknowledgments

The greatest thank-you goes to my publisher, Edward Jutkowitz, for letting me put my obsession on paper. Thanks also to my editor, Gregg Wilhelm, who tamed my enthusiasm, harnessed my vision, and perfected my prose.

A travel guide without maps is like a Chesapeake Bay crab cake without Old Bay. I don't do maps, but am fortunate to have a great friend who does. Thank you, Susan Tseng, for crafting graphics that are precise and lucid.

A profound thank-you goes out to my family on so many levels. To my wife Kelly: thanks for helping unleash my latent wanderlust; for sharing in my infectious quest for discovery; for accepting my writing this book—truly a labor of love—with unremitting patience; and for hoofing over one hundred miles with me on fact-checking missions. To my daughter Zi Li and son Graham: thank you for joining daddy on hikes when you could, and for being understanding when you couldn't. You both deserve a popsicle. And to my mom Lucille and sister Renee: thanks for sharing and encouraging the Strzelecki family's thirst for travel and exploration.

Though many folks contributed to the content of this book, several went beyond what was expected and deserve special mention. Meg Fielding showed me Roland Park from an insider's vantage. Scott Shead, Jim Neill, and Nancy Branucci proved that beneath Locust Point's blue-collar veneer is a wonderful and fascinating community.

Many thanks to those friends who helped "test drive" my hikes by weathering not only the miles, but also my prattling commentary. They include David Bushey, William H. Bushey, William P. Bushey, Karen Kuszyk, Todd Kuszyk, Sarah Montgomery, Rhea Montgomery-Walsh, Vivian Montgomery-Walsh, Eric Osnes, Jennifer Staraska, Adrian Vaughan, Brendan Vaughan, Kathleen Vaughan, Ariana Wall, Judy Wall, Julia Wall, Michael Wall, and Daryl Walsh.

Additional thanks to Kathleen Dias, Rich McGuire, Sarah Montgomery, John Smith, Judy Wall, and Daryl Montgomery for proofreading assistance.

About the Hiker

Mike Strzelecki is a technical writer by trade, a travel writer by avocation, and an urban wanderer. He has hiked many of the world's great cities, and considers Baltimore among that group. He is also the author of *Baltimore with Children;* writes the "Focus on Fathers" column for *Baltimore's Child* magazine; is a contributor to *Running Through the Wall,* edited by Neal Jamison; and has been published in *The Sun, Blue Ridge Country, Central PA, Pennsylvania, Running Times, Trail Runner, Ultrarunning,* and *Runner's Gazette.* He resides in Catonsville, Maryland, with his wife and children.

Corrections

Things change. Restaurants open and close. Monuments are built and museums shut their doors. Inaccuracies creep into literature. So that future editions of *Urban Hikes In and Around Baltimore* will be as accurate as possible, please send any corrections from this edition to:

Urban Hikes
c/o Camino Books
P.O. Box 59026
Philadelphia, PA 19102

or e-mail the author at: gramzili@bcpl.net

Index

Of Related Interest

Baltimore with Children
Mike Strzelecki

With this guidebook handy, parents will have no trouble planning exciting excursions in Baltimore—from Agritainment to Zoos—all field-tested by the author's own young daughter and son. More than a list with just the facts, *Baltimore with Children* provides detailed descriptions of each attraction, steering patents to the unexpected delights of a tire park, a store that caters to budding magicians, and a café with the (mechanical) alligator lurking in a wishing pond, among other enticements.

The Original Baltimore Neighborhood Cookbook
Irina Smith and Ann Hazan

What better way to acquaint yourself with Baltimore than through the spirit of treasured family recipes? To make their collection for this book, the authors traveled miles by car and on foot to taste and test the favorites of people in over fifty Baltimore neighborhoods. The easy-to-follow recipes are complete with serving suggestions and commentary, so you can now enjoy these one-of-a-kind dishes in your own home.

CAMINO BOOKS, INC.
P. O. Box 59026
Philadelphia, PA 19102
www.caminobooks.com

Please send me:

_____ copy(ies) of *Urban Hikes In and Around Baltimore*, $14.95

_____ copy(ies) of *Baltimore with Children*, $16.95

_____ copy(ies) of *The Original Baltimore Neighborhood Cookbook*, $16.95

Name: _____

Address: _____

City/State/Zip: _____

All orders must be prepaid. Your satisfaction is guaranteed. You may return the books for a full refund. Please add $5.95 for postage and handling for the first book and $1.00 for each additional.

84-8